Endorsements

"I was captivated by this real life story of a family's faith that perseveres. This is an amazing story still being written, a must read for those who desire to fully embrace an orphan's love."

ROD VESTAL
Former Campus/Community Missions Pastor, Lake Pointe Church
Previously served with World Orphans

"This is a heartfelt story of faithfulness to God's plan during difficult and uncertain times, showing how God can ultimately use you to bless the lives of others and be blessed as well, even when each step along the way is unclear. I recommend this inspirational book to adoptive families and to anyone who has faced difficulties when responding to God's calling."

ANDREW STEELE
Former Adoption and Foster Care Ministry Lead
Lake Pointe Church

"Within the pages of Rachelle's story, one hears her despair and brokenness. It is in this time of brokenness that God revealed another plan—his plan. Hemingway said, 'Life breaks us all, and afterwards, some are strong at the broken places.' You will be blessed by this story which offers the best of what life has to teach us by giving the broken pieces to a God who sees the bigger picture of our lives.'"

SIMONE MONROE
Women's Minister
Lake Pointe Church

Reader Reviews

"I loved God's abundant love for your family. It reminds me of the old hymn; THIS IS MY STORY, THIS IS MY SONG, PRAISING MY SAVIOR ALL THE DAY LONG. God took your story and turned it into a song."

DAN GREENER, CO

"Inspirational."

GENNY TATIANA, OLIVA, TX

"Loved how vulnerable you were and transparent to the reader but in all of this, you gave God the glory by clinging to HIM and HIS word for your strength, wisdom, patience, guidance and most of all HIS abundant love. Thanks for sharing your story."

CAROL GREENER, CO

"God used your story and your poems to minister to me when and how I needed it. The poem "How Would I Know" was beautiful. When I finished I journaled and used your same structure and theme to write a prayer of gratitude to God. It was a very special time and I'm so thankful for it."

MELODY WALKER, BOGOTÁ, COLOMBIA

"Thank you for writing your story. I am sure that I am not the only one to be blessed by it."

KELLY BASALO, IN

SURVIVING THE VALLEY · BOOK ONE

Unexpected Tears

TRUSTING GOD THROUGH A PAINFUL ADOPTION PROCESS

Rachelle D. Alspaugh

AUTHENTICITY
BOOK HOUSE

Copyright © 2015 by Rachelle D. Alspaugh
ISBN: 978-1-943004-71-3

This book was previously published as *From the Mountain... to the Valley... and Back!*

Most names have been changed throughout the book to protect the rights of those not legally connected to the family or who could not give permission to use their name. The following names are the actual names of the characters in the story: Mike, Rachelle, David, Juan David, and Julian.

All rights reserved. No part of this book may be used or reproduced by any means, graphic, electronic, or mechanical, including photocopying, recording, taping or by any information storage retrieval system without the written permission of the publisher except in the case of brief quotations embodied in critical articles and reviews.

All Scripture quotations, unless otherwise indicated, are taken from the Holy Bible: *New International* Version©. NIV©. Copyright © 1973, 1978, 1984 by International Bible Society. Used by permission of Zondervan. All rights reserved.

Scripture quotations marked "ESV" are taken from The Holy Bible: English Standard Version, copyright 2001, Wheaton: Good News Publishers. Used by permission. All rights reserved.

Because of the dynamic nature of the Internet, any web addresses or links contained in this book may have changed since publication and may no longer be valid.

Published by Authenticity Book House

Printed in the United States of America

10 9 8 7 6 5 4 3 2 1

Authenticity Book House
c/o Proven Way Ministries
The Hope Center
2001 W. Plano Parkway, Suite 3422
Plano, TX 75075 USA

Dedication

I dedicate this book to:
Yo dedico este libro a:

My two boys, my biological son and my Colombian "son,"
David and Julian—You are both a miracle to me.
Mis dos hijos, mi hijo biológico y mi "hijo" colombiano, David y
Julian—Los dos son un milagro a mí.

Juan David and Viviana, you will always have my heart.
Juan David y Viviana, siempre tendrán mi corazón.

Clarita, I'm so glad God dropped us off on your doorstep.
Thanks for taking us in.

Table of Contents

Introduction 1

PART ONE—From the Mountain … 3

    Chapter One—Called to Adopt 5

    Chapter Two—Following God's Lead 21

    Chapter Three—God's Endless Provisions 33

    Chapter Four—Beginning to Bond 39

    Chapter Five—Longing for My Children 51

    Chapter Six—An Answer We Didn't Expect 63

PART TWO—To the Valley… 81

    Chapter Seven—Falling Apart 83

    Chapter Eight—Grieving 97

    Chapter Nine—Emptiness 113

PART THREE—And Back! 121

    Chapter Ten—Latching onto Hope 123

    Chapter Eleven—Experiencing His Grace 137

    Chapter Twelve— Understanding His Purpose 147

    Chapter Thirteen—Understanding His Plan 157

    Chapter Fourteen—United at Last 171

    Epilogue 183

    Appendix 187

Introduction

God sets desires deep inside us early in life to guide us in the direction of his will. Even as a young preteen, I hoped to one day mother someone else's child. A calling to adopt gripped my heart, along with a desire to become bilingual and to work on a mission field.

Because I grew up a pastor's daughter, my church pretty much raised me. I found myself at church every time the doors opened. We arrived first and left last, not missing a single service, prayer meeting, choir practice, or youth activity. Obviously, the scriptures imbedded themselves in my heart at a young age, but I still vividly remember the missionary stories read to us during the children's church hour. They fascinated me, captivated me. I held on to every little detail. Someday I hoped I might have my own missionary story to write.

Though my dad's salary as a pastor left no room for traveling adventures outside the United States, I somehow developed a love for and fascination with other cultures, places, and ways of living. The American Dream bored me. To me, it represented an empty life, void of real meaning or adventure.

I took Spanish classes through middle and high school and fell in love with the language. I used it often with any of my Spanish-speaking contacts. My yearning to speak Spanish fluently led me to Buenos Aires, Argentina, to study abroad the first semester of my junior year in college. I lived with an amazing Christian family, attended a wonderful church, and studied Spanish in a university among a group of international students from all around the world. The experience changed me forever.

Six months after coming home from Argentina, my fiancé, Mike, and I spent a summer in Mexico living and working with missionary friends. Mike performed maintenance duties for a Bible camp while I helped the campers and taught English classes in the community. God used that unforgettable experience to show me how he fulfills the desires of our heart when we allow him to set those desires within us.

In 1999, I graduated from Grace College in Winona Lake, Indiana, with a degree in Christian Ministries and a minor in Spanish. I dreamed of one day teaching English overseas, preferably in a Spanish-speaking country. A few months later, I married my high school sweetheart, who shared similar desires for the mission field. Two years after the wedding, our son, David, entered our world, making us a family of three. It didn't take me long after his birth to plan out our life together.

Oh, I had so much to learn. Mountain top experiences awaited us as a new family pursuing our dreams, as well as deep valleys that left us clinging to God for our very existence. While following our calling to adopt, we fell in love with two precious orphans. The desire to adopt these sweet children brought unexpected tears at every turn, taking us into a deep valley we never expected and one we never wanted to travel. This story describes our survival through that valley, a journey filled with a beauty more breathtaking than we ever imagined.

> "No eye has seen, no ear has heard, no mind has conceived what God has prepared for those who love him."
> 1 Corinthians 2:9

Part One
FROM THE MOUNTAIN...

CALLED TO ADOPT

"In the morning, O Lord, you hear my voice; in the morning I lay my requests before you and wait in expectation."
Psalm 5:3

Who Will Carry a Sibling for My Son?

How deeply I've longed for
a sibling for my son.
My dream has always been
a foreign adoption.

I see a Latin child
linking hands with a white,
both speaking in Spanish
and English all night.

It seemed impossible
until this recent year.
A possibility
now so very clear.

Anxiously awaiting
a chance to save for her.
My dream so tangible—
how excited we were!

Yet one day all that changed
when I found out that I
now held within me
a dream we let die.

Our hearts quickly changed,
envisioning our child—
what we'd least expected
made my thinking run wild!

I felt total peace,
it all seemed so right.
Things fell right into place.
Our baby now in sight!

I never imagined
how short-lived it could be.
I never expected
I would lose this baby.

I couldn't believe it,
would God play with my heart?
Why would he tease us,
and tear our dreams apart?

Now I'm left wond'ring if,
while back here at square one,
I'm the one to carry
a sibling for my son.

Grief. I expected it to last longer. Though completely unplanned and unexpected, this pregnancy seemed so timely. Details fell into place as soon as we shared our news. A late November birth would work well with a school schedule, allowing me both a time off for maternity leave, as well as a few extra weeks with the Christmas holiday. Two people offered us quality, affordable daycare within only a few days.

Yet as quickly as we discovered the pregnancy, God took our new baby home. I suffered a miscarriage a few weeks later.

"Our baby got sick, so sick we could never take care of it. God took our baby to Heaven to wait for us there." The tears still welled up in our little boy's eyes despite my attempt to explain the miscarriage. He'd just lost his first sibling, and it affected him more deeply than I understood at the time. We all struggled with the initial shock over the abrupt ending to our pregnancy.

I took a day off work to spend some time alone. After several hours in one of my favorite coffee shops, with a soothing drink and a notebook, I heard God speak to me so clearly through my poetry.

"Your child already lives and waits for you." A simple phrase from Heaven touched me deeply.

I left that coffee shop with peace in my heart rather than the heavy grief I arrived with a few hours earlier. More than peace, I felt an inexplicable joy. The time came to begin our adoption journey.

Six months later, we found ourselves sitting through an adoption conference our church advertised for months.

"I can barely contain my excitement! Your time has arrived! We are finally here!" I silently screamed of my enthusiasm to God, but I really wanted to climb on the roof and shout it out for all to hear. Okay, so that's not really my personality, but I could hardly believe it when the day finally arrived.

I dreamed my whole life to adopt a foreign child, yet I nearly lost sight of my dream over the last few years. The opportunity now stood before us as a couple, and we embraced it. We listened to each speaker at the conference tell their own story of adoption, extinguishing our fears of the unknown. What once seemed impossible and overwhelming now held possibility. We both sensed God's obvious timing to begin our adoption journey.

Over the lunch hour, my husband, Mike, and I joined another couple at a table, and we shared our reasons for coming to the conference.

"So what brings you here today?" I asked, almost assuming everyone came with the same enthusiasm.

"We've struggled with infertility for years. We've spent so much money on so many doctors, treatments, and procedures, but nothing seems to work. I don't know if I'm ready to think about adoption yet, but we're here to check it out." She desperately wanted to bear a child of her own and didn't feel ready to give up trying. For her, adoption meant defeat, having to accept Plan B. God had not yet placed the desire on her heart.

We, on the other hand, never once felt even a twinge of desire to look into fertility options as a couple. God already blessed us with the biological birth of our son, David, six years earlier. We grieved the miscarriage of our second pregnancy, but we did not long to bear more children of our own. Too many children lived without the love and security of a family. We both felt God would grow our family through adoption someday.

Our marriage started off much rockier than we imagined. During the first few years, we had to scrape our way through a series of financial disasters that kept us from even envisioning an adoption process any earlier. Now, upon seeing the anguish written on this woman's face over a decision to adopt, and at the same time feeling incredible excitement over our own decision confirmed God's timing for us.

I felt like I stood on top of the mountain that day, yet quite a distance still separated us from the mountain. We'd only taken a few steps in that direction.

After the lunch hour, we specifically attended a presentation by an adoption agency starting a brand new program in El Salvador. We wanted a little girl from a Spanish-speaking country so we could continue to raise her in a bilingual home. We'd watched our son build a sweet friendship with a girl his age, so we thought maybe a sister close in age to him would fit well in our family. After we sat through the entire session and found how to get started, we felt convinced God led us directly to this program.

"A complete process to adopt from El Salvador should take about eighteen months, and then you will spend about three weeks in the country before bringing your child home." The presenter's predictions sounded completely doable and also like a wonderful travel opportunity. I could hardly wait! The excitement brewed within me.

By attending the conference that day, we found a Christian agency, picked a country, talked with a representative, and walked out with the application in hand. We didn't even stay around for the rest of the day's events. We left early to pick up David from a babysitter, and I completed our application online before I even made it to bed that night.

I sent an e-mail to my mom to tell her we'd finally begun the process to adopt an international child. Knowing the desire God put on my heart many years earlier, she responded, "It's about time!"

I couldn't agree more with her. I dreamed of the day I'd meet my princess, my daughter, in El Salvador.

Soon after applying though, we found out the process would actually take at least two full years, if not more. The El Salvador program was a new program, still in the works, with several test families still in their own process. The longer wait time didn't bother us since it gave us more time to save money for all of the expenses involved. Expenses we couldn't even fathom at the time.

Oh, did we have a lot to learn about international adoption! We didn't have a clue. We took our time gathering all the necessary paperwork for our home study, the first step in a long, tedious, overwhelming process.

Several months passed while the piles of paperwork grew higher. We wrote our testimonies and expressed our desires to adopt. We recorded every detail of our finances on paper. Several friends and family members answered questionnaires about us. Meanwhile we saved money like crazy to pay for this first step.

Finally, after about six months, we saved enough money to turn it all in to our agency. A social worker could now arrange the first of three required visits to complete our home study.

Throughout those six months, I researched the present orphan crisis in El Salvador, and I joined several online adoption groups. I wanted to know more about the process from others who either walked this road in the past or currently walked it with us. I loved reading everyone's stories, their reasons for wanting to adopt, and specifically why they chose El Salvador. They inspired me.

I soon connected closely with another member of the group and formed an instant bond with her. We shared several things in common, including our teaching experience in the bilingual/ESL field and our experiences studying abroad in college. We both desired to bring up bilingual children. Mike and I never desired to look into fertility options because we always felt called to adopt someday. My new friend and her husband felt called to pursue adoption first before ever finding out if they could have biological children.

So thankful to find this friendship, she and I encouraged and prayed for one another via e-mail. We never actually met because we lived on opposite sides of the country, but that instant connection grew into a friendship I still cherish to this day, several years later.

However, following the online group actually left me more discouraged every day. I quickly learned the program with El Salvador never truly established itself the way the agency hoped and expected. By reading online how other couples struggled and how long they'd already been in the program, I realized this process could last for years. Bitterness already took root among those who began their process more than two years earlier with still no progress in sight.

Did God truly call us to this program and this country? Did our child already await us there? These questions weighed heavily on my heart, but we continued to collect the necessary paperwork and funds to continue.

Our social worker soon contacted us to set up the first of three meetings with her. In two weeks, we'd meet at a local coffee shop. Things progressed, despite my change of heart and the new uncertainties about this decision.

One morning during those two weeks, I spent a long morning alone with God out on my front porch. (I cherish that luxury of time during the summer while my husband works and my son sleeps the morning away.) Those questions burdened my heart and mind that morning as I tearfully poured out my concerns to God. I'd lost all sense of peace over this being his direction. Adopting a child from El Salvador looked more impossible every day. We felt so sure God led us to that specific agency and country, but I now felt almost foolish to even consider continuing in that direction.

"Father, if our child truly awaits us in El Salvador, then we will plunge ourselves into this process and pour out every penny necessary until you choose to unite us with her." (We'd requested a girl between the ages of three and seven, close in age to David.) "But if our child waits somewhere else, please show us." I waited expectantly for more guidance.

As I finished my morning time of prayer, I went inside. David still slept soundly in his bed, so I sat down at the computer in the spare bedroom to check my e-mail. I browsed through several new messages, and one in particular caught my eye regarding the chance to meet an older child from Colombia who needed a family.

I remembered inquiring recently about an organization that brings older orphans from Colombia for a summer hosting program, so I opened the e-mail to find out more about the actual kids coming.

Their ages normally ranged from nine to fourteen years old, and they would stay in the United States for five weeks in order to experience life with a family. The program welcomes visiting families to come meet the children, hoping one will consider becoming a forever family to each child. The kids stayed with families in cities all over the States, but fourteen of them would soon reside in Austin, Texas, only a few hours away from us. This e-mail included photos of all fourteen of them.

To be honest, the ages of the kids didn't speak to me since we already set our hearts on a girl close in age to our son. I glanced through the pictures anyway, looking specifically for a five- or six-year-old girl. By the time my eyes reached the bottom of the page, a picture of a six-year-old little girl, Viviana, stared back at me, almost locking my eyes with hers.

I couldn't take my eyes off of her. "Is this your answer, God? Could she be the child waiting for us?"

I read her short biography and description, and I soon found out she came with a sibling, her ten-year-old brother, Juan David. They wanted nothing more than to be adopted—together, of course.

Mike and I never discussed adopting siblings, nor had we even considered a boy, especially one older than David. But something kept tugging at my heart, so I glanced at his biography, too. Wow. He and David shared many things in common, including a birthday month and a passion to play soccer. He also loved and excelled in Math, the area where David already showed obvious talent, even at the age of six.

"Could this be, God? Two of them?" My mind raced with possibilities.

I mentioned the idea to David later that day while he played in his bedroom. "What if we adopted a boy and a girl together?"

He wasn't against the idea until I mentioned Juan David's age. "No. No. No. I want to stay the oldest. I don't want a brother older than me. No. Not gonna happen."

But, as the day went on, I couldn't get those two siblings off my mind. David and I talked off and on throughout the day about it. I mentioned things he already had in common with Juan David. We discussed the adventure of playing soccer in the yard with his big brother every day after school. I could stay inside to play with dolls and do hair with Viviana, while Juan David showed David all the cool soccer moves they do in Colombia.

The more I talked it up, the more his heart softened to the idea. In fact, he even jokingly asked me a few days later if we could adopt Juan David and not Viviana. God continued to work on him.

After I shared my thoughts with Mike, his openness surprised me. "Wherever God leads, we'll go."

I printed out those two little pictures and put them on the refrigerator. We prayed for both of them every day after that.

By the end of the week, David and I went on a little date together to our favorite restaurant. While we ate, he looked up at me and said, "Mommy, do you love them?"

I looked into his little six-year-old eyes and said, "Yes, Sweetheart, I do. I pray for them every day, and I can truly say I already love them."

With more maturity than I even knew that little boy possessed, he looked back into my eyes and said, "Then we better go down to meet them before someone else does."

Now, we'd only ever visited Austin once, we weren't familiar with the area, and we didn't know anyone who lived there. We didn't have any wiggle room financially since we'd already poured out a few thousand dollars to start our home study for our El Salvador adoption process. I didn't exactly budget for a random weekend trip to Austin.

But I did remember receiving an e-mail about a week or so earlier from a dear friend who recently moved to Round Rock, inviting any friends to come visit when they travel through the area. She raved about the prime location of their home right outside of Austin! I call that divine timing.

"Thank you, God!" I quickly replied to her message, explained the situation, and asked if we could visit them one of the weekends with activities scheduled for the Colombian kids to meet visiting families. My friend was so excited for us that she said we could come two weeks later for the kids' second weekend event.

God awed me with his guidance and provision. We'd get to meet the kids and also spend quality time with our friends who moved away. He opened wide the door and said, "Go. Those children are waiting for you."

For two weeks, I longed to meet those two kids. We prayed for them every day. However, we continued with our El Salvador adoption process until God made it clear we needed to stop. We met with our social worker a week later, survived our first interview, and scheduled our second visit about three weeks later. We did mention our upcoming opportunity to meet two Colombian kids the following week, so we let her know in our first visit that our plans might change.

I nearly went crazy that last week as I waited to meet those two precious children who captured our hearts. However, we kept pretty quiet about it. We wanted to see for ourselves where God might take this without involving anyone else's thoughts or opinions. Our friends in Round Rock used to attend a small group meeting with us, so we couldn't help but spill our news when we told the other group members who we planned to stay with for the weekend.

We had no idea what outcome the visit might bring, but we knew we at least needed to go see. We simply had to meet this brother and sister from Colombia. We'd already seen too many connections to even try to ignore them. Our friends from our small group agreed and literally bathed us in prayer over the next week. We didn't know what to expect, but at least it might confirm whether or not we needed to stay in the El Salvador program.

We left home on Saturday morning, June 19, to head to Round Rock. On the way down, Mike and I used the time to talk about what might come next if we still felt the same after meeting these kids.

"So, what if things go well this weekend and we want to spend more time with the kids?" I looked toward Mike to read his facial expression when he heard my question.

"Then I guess we'll just come back next weekend, too." Mike's reply actually surprised me, while at the same time confirming God's tug on both of our hearts.

What a weekend we had ahead of us. There's nothing better than celebrating a great reunion with friends. After enjoying an amazing dinner together, we stayed up late playing games, talking and laughing for hours. We'd traveled to Mexico with them two times in the last five years, so a lot of memories came back!

The following afternoon, July 20, we all headed to the lake together for an activity with the Colombian kids. The hosting program arranged a special day for the kids to celebrate Colombia's Independence Day by letting them swim, play, and enjoy a big picnic.

I'll never forget the moment I finally laid eyes on that little girl. I spotted her immediately in the shallow area of the water. My heart skipped a beat, and I instantly fell in love. She had no idea of the connection between us before I said hello.

We introduced ourselves to one of the people in charge, and we expressed our desire to specifically meet Viviana and Juan David.

"That's so great you came all this way to meet these kids! You should try to get to know several of the kids because there's always a chance their hosting family will decide to adopt them." Her advice made sense.

Mike and I glanced quickly at each other and shook our heads.

"You know, we only feel a tug on our hearts for these specific siblings, Juan David and Viviana." They already claimed our hearts. We agreed we didn't feel pulled toward any of the other children.

The coordinator then introduced us to the couple hosting

Juan David and Viviana for the summer, and we sat and talked with them for a while. They told us what they knew so far about the kids and their history.

"They have an older half-brother, Julian, but apparently he's not adoptable. He just wants his siblings to be adopted together. They all live in the same orphanage, but in different homes." They talked more about the kids' personalities and preferences while we all sat watching them play in the water.

David didn't want to play in the water alone, so Mike and I got in with him for a little bit. He took his soccer ball to toss back and forth, and before we knew it, we'd inched our way close to Viviana and tossed the ball to her. What a surreal moment to realize the little girl from the picture on my refrigerator stood right in front of me, tossing a soccer ball back and forth with David in the water. When I later printed out the picture I'd snapped of the two of them, I couldn't help but wonder if it represented our first picture of David and his little sister.

Juan David swam in the deeper part of the lake with the majority of the older kids. We interacted very little with him while in the water, but we stole a chance to talk with him by the picnic table at dinner time while he devoured hot dog after hot dog. He and I talked about his school, his class, his birthday, and his love of math and soccer. An outgoing child, he enjoyed every minute playing in the water with other kids close to his age, eager to meet so many new people.

Pretty quickly after eating, all the kids jumped back into the water. I knew I wanted to come back the following week to get to know these kids even more, but I hadn't said anything to Mike yet, nor had he said anything to me.

Before we even found a chance to talk about it, the man hosting the children asked if we'd like to come back the following weekend to spend some more focused time alone with those two.

"You know, we'd love that!" We both quickly agreed.

"Okay, then why don't we meet for lunch next Saturday before the bowling event? Maybe we can arrange a picnic or something to give you a chance to talk with the kids." He said he'd stay in touch via e-mail sometime during the week to work out the details.

"Okay, God, could this get any easier or work out any better? Thank you!" The pieces almost naturally connected to make this work.

Although the couple considered the thought of adopting them, they could see these kids would fit well into our family—Juan David, with his soccer and math in common with David (at the time, Mike even coached David's soccer team, too), and only a few months separated David and Viviana in age. She showed a definite need for extra attention in school, so my occupation as a bilingual teacher a grade level above her could only serve as a huge benefit to her.

Another family also sparked up a conversation with us later in the day. "So, you guys came all the way from Dallas for this?"

"You know, those little pictures just kept tugging on our hearts ever since we saw them. We came down just to see."

Only a year earlier, they, too, visited an activity for the same reason. Now they sat across from us with their recently adopted son. Wow. Would we follow in their footsteps?

The day soon came to a close, and we headed back to our friends' house to gather our things and say good-bye. They rejoiced with us over our invitation to return the following weekend, graciously extending the offer to stay with them again. God showed us his provisions from the start. Now I needed to patiently wait yet another whole week before I could see those precious children again.

The coordinator of the event contacted me throughout the week to find out our thoughts and intentions now after meeting the kids. She said we needed to write up a letter of intent if we seriously wanted the opportunity to pursue their adoption. A letter as such only put us in line for them to call us if their host family did not choose to seek an adoption. We spent the next few days working together on our letter, and we corresponded via e-mail with the kids' host parents to arrange details for the following weekend.

We didn't want to seem pushy, selfish, or overbearing with our desire to know these kids while they, too, wanted to cherish every moment with them as they pondered over their own decision. It felt a little awkward at times, but they made us feel comfortable and appreciated.

"Hey, we feel like the more people who love them, the better chances they have to gain a family." They obviously shared one goal.

We returned the following weekend, this time covered in prayer by everyone we knew. No secrets this time. We knew the clear wisdom and guidance we desired could only be found through prayer. We suspected God's plan to entirely change our direction and lead us onto a new path, thus turning our lives completely upside down.

First we met up with the kids and their host "dad" in the home they stayed in that summer. They eagerly showed us their summer beds, some of their toys, and the clothes given to them for their stay. They quickly changed into their swimming attire before we all headed out to play in a nearby park with water fountains.

The two kids splashed around in the water with David for a long while, playing in the fountains and enjoying being wet. Later, we all stood over a little bridge and quietly observed the fish and turtles in the water below. The turtles captivated Juan David's attention. I didn't know it, but Mike snapped a picture of me standing there with David, Juan David, and Viviana—a picture I cherished for many months as the first picture of me and my three children.

We all grew more comfortable together throughout the day. Later, after everyone dried off, we embraced the opportunity to show the kids some pictures we'd brought of our life in Dallas, including David's soccer pictures.

"Someday I want to play on a team like that." I tucked Juan David's comment away in my heart, silently vowing to make sure that happened if we could adopt them. I so loved this child already.

After spending an hour together over lunch, talking and observing the kids' personalities, we headed to the bowling alley to join the other Colombian children. I loved teaching Juan David how to bowl, and Mike snapped several pictures. (None of those kids ever bowled before, and they didn't have a clue what to do.) We only took a few pictures that day, but we did capture several precious moments, including a snapshot of David sitting at a table with both Juan David and Viviana. A picture always meant to be.

The time passed way too quickly that day before we said good-bye. One more weekend remained until the kids returned to Colombia, but I already knew we couldn't make it back. We already planned to travel to my parents' house in another state. We returned home, fell on our knees, and prayed, mainly for wisdom for their host family to know who should pursue their adoption. Apparently, other families also expressed interest in this sibling pair.

I hadn't guarded my heart a bit. Those pictures on my refrigerator came to life, and I fell completely in love.

As soon as we got home, we called our social worker to put the El Salvador adoption on hold until further notice.

FOLLOWING GOD'S LEAD

"Whether you turn to the right or to the left, your ears will hear a voice behind you, saying, 'This is the way; walk in it.'"
Isaiah 30:21

Could Those Be My Children?

A simple summer awaited us,
A few months of peace and rest,
A chance to finish up paperwork
for the child with whom we'd be blessed.

Yet such peace wouldn't surround me,
Neither to continue our process nor to stop.
I felt no sense of direction,
I begged for an answer to drop.

Within minutes of uttering my teary prayer,
I found two little faces on my computer screen.
A sibling pair from Colombia,
A little girl and a male preteen.

My heart immediately drew my attention
to the question now on my mind.
Could those be my children?
Was this the answer I sought to find?

We began to pray for them daily.
They soon became a part of us.
We made arrangements to meet them,
surprised at how easy it was.

Everything went so smoothly
from planning to actually meeting face to face.
God granted us favor in the eyes of so many.
We knew we stood in our appointed place.

We fell in love with the children
and can already envision them as our own.
Obstacles still stand around us,
yet in my heart such hope has grown.

For the moment I'm at peace
as I wait for an answer from above.
I pray for strength in whatever outcome,
as I stare at their faces, completely in love.

If these are not my children
I know somehow they are part of the plan.
He brought them down my path for a reason
So on that hope I continue to stand.

How in the world do you go home to sit and wait after such an experience? God turned our lives upside down in less than ten days. Wow. We prayed constantly, daily putting those children back in his hands. We knew our God had a definite plan for their adoption. For some reason he let our paths cross at this precise time in our adoption journey.

Thankfully, David and I already planned a trip up North less than a week later to visit several family members and friends, so packing and making final arrangements preoccupied me. We wouldn't hear from anyone for several weeks, anyway, so I thanked God for the distraction.

Our trip included several stops, starting with my parents' home. Then we planned to meet up with my brother and sister-in-law who lived a few hours away to stay with them for a few days. After that, the four of us would travel a few more hours to visit Mike's parents. David and I made arrangements to stay there so we could attend a *Quinceañera* for a previous ESL student I'd worked with as a kindergartener. (A Quinceañera is a special fifteenth birthday celebration significant for females in Latin American culture.) I taught many of the girl's siblings and cousins, too, so her family held a special place in my heart. The invitation honored me.

Plenty of activity kept me occupied while we waited. Sadly, Mike's work schedule did not allow him to join us. I wanted to take advantage of this trip to love on David like crazy in case God did plan to add these two children to our family.

We settled at my parents' house and enjoyed a relaxing time playing games and making crafts. (My mom's house resembles a craft-making haven. She's incredibly gifted with her hands, and her unfinished basement allows her to store all kinds of supplies. It's one of my favorite things to do whenever we visit.) While there, I worked on crafting a special gift to take to the Quinceañera.

I did rather well with the "waiting," so the e-mail from the summer events' coordinator surprised me when it arrived after only a few short days rather than the weeks I expected.

"We talked extensively with the kids' host family, and we agree your family seems the best match for these children. You are free to pursue their adoption if you still want to."

If we still wanted to? Of course, we did! I felt like jumping up and down with excitement! Instead, I called Mike to share our wonderful news.

"Mike, they chose us as the best fit for the kids! We can start the process to adopt them! They really are our children!"

Even though we hadn't even started the adoption process, this e-mail confirmed in our hearts God chose these children for us. Our child did not await us in El Salvador. Our children resided in Austin, Texas, at that moment and would soon return to Colombia to wait for us.

The coordinator also asked us to come back again that weekend to spend more time with the kids and meet the social worker who came with them. She wanted to get to know us and observe our interactions with both children, something we later realized she should have done the previous two weekends.

Sadly, we couldn't make it work since we already traveled to another state. She gave me the social worker's phone number and asked me to tell her about our ambitions to adopt a child and what drew us to these kids. Since we'd never met, the conversation felt pretty awkward.

"Without meeting you and watching you interact with the kids, there's really no need for us to talk. But don't worry. Colombia's decision to approve your adoption isn't based on what I say about you, anyway. It just helps get you off on the right start."

Soon a whirlwind of internet activity, e-mails, and phone calls with the coordinator dominated my time at my parents' home as she tried to guide us through our next steps. First, we needed to find an agency. She gave me a list of about five different agencies in the United States that worked directly with the summer hosting organization so the adopting parents still ended up with the same child they started with. (Most adoption processes direct you through the entire process before they match you with a specific child).

Since none of the agencies were in Texas, we chose the agency the coordinator used previously for her own adoption. She successfully adopted her daughter through them, so we hoped for the same outcome in our case. I contacted the agency right away, and they immediately mailed the application packet to our home.

We also needed to completely back out of the El Salvador program. Our contact person understood, seeing how God clearly led us to these two Colombian children.

"Your social worker will just need to change her interview questions to make your home study reflect a Colombian adoption rather than an El Salvador one. Since you've already paid the entire fee and met once already, it will save you a lot of time and money to stay with the same social worker."

That made perfect sense, so I called the social worker and left a message explaining our new situation. I said I would call her again when I returned from vacation so we could set up our next visit as soon as possible.

However, before jumping completely into the process, we needed to write a new letter of intent to the Colombian government (a petition to specifically adopt Juan David and Viviana). It required exact wording in several places, an explanation of our own desire and intent, and extensive information about ourselves and our family history, plus someone needed to write it in Spanish. We could not send it until after the kids returned to the orphanage in Colombia for a specified amount of time. Our process could officially begin once we received a reply.

This gave us a few weeks to get everything ready to prevent any delays once we gained permission to begin the process. We knew those were our children. We prepared ourselves for whatever it took to adopt them and bring them home.

My heart overflowed with joy for the remainder of our vacation up North. I printed out a few pictures we'd taken of my future son and daughter and carried them around with me wherever I went. While in Indiana for our last few days, I met with several friends at my favorite coffee shop. I can't even describe how wonderful it felt each time I shared those pictures of my future children. Nothing could stop me from bringing them home.

Other families we met in Austin told us the process normally took about ten months at the most. Many took even less time! We started our home study process a few weeks earlier, so I assumed we might already be ahead.

Mike handed me the package from our new adoption agency as soon as David and I arrived home after our trip. Inside that package, I found applications, instructions, timelines, and lists of every necessary document. I also noted which ones to notarize and which ones to apostille, or properly authenticate, by the states they came from.

Then I read even more instructions on how to apostille our documents, plus I found tips from other people who adopted from Colombia in the past. Tips on what to do and not do during the process, how to speed up parts of the paper chase, and tips on travel and residing in Colombia (most families stayed between four to six weeks in the country with the child while waiting for the paperwork to pass through all the courts). The packet also included a few success stories. As I read them, I imagined our own success story included in someone else's adoption packet someday.

We composed our letter to the Colombian government stating our petition to adopt Juan David and Viviana. I speak fluent enough Spanish to teach bilingual education and to travel and communicate with ease, but I did not trust my Spanish to write such a formal letter. I asked some friends to translate it for us, and then they asked a Colombian friend to make sure it looked and sounded okay.

Once the kids returned to their country for a specified amount of time, we sent the letter to Colombia via DHL. Wow. How quickly we found out that a huge portion of expenses in an international adoption goes toward postage and airmail.

An e-mail response from Colombia came fairly quickly, asking for more information concerning family history issues that led us to counseling in the earlier years of our marriage. However, the actual counselor we saw had since moved and left no address or contact information with anyone. After sending a few e-mails back and forth with this first contact in Colombia, and making an appointment with a new counselor, we gained permission to proceed with the adoption process as long as we addressed the issue in detail in the required psychological evaluation later.

Now officially in the process, we immediately faced problems. My summer vacation quickly came to a close, making all my "free time" disappear. This impeded the speed of how much paperwork we accomplished each day, and it made doing so much more stressful than when I still had summer hours to work on it at home.

We started our application with the new adoption agency first, which required half of the agency fees up front: $2,225. This depleted our adoption savings thus far, since our previous adoption plan gave us more time to save. The rest of this adoption meant a complete walk of faith, one step at a time. We knew many organizations offered financial aid for adoptions, so we immediately started applying for as much help as possible. We went by word of mouth recommendations, and we researched online for as many organizations as we could find.

Completing a dossier for an international adoption is a tedious, time-consuming process that will challenge even your sanity at times. Piles of papers occupied our desk, each requiring a similar yet distinct list of forms. Documents accumulated for the agency's checklist, mostly originals which cost a small fortune to acquire. Other stacks of forms needed to be copied and notarized. Different financial aid applications requested even more paperwork. Our home study still lacked a few documents, plus we needed to make copies of everything for our own files.

I often wondered what in the world we'd gotten ourselves into. Yet one glance at those beautiful faces in the pictures now hanging all over the place gave me a new burst of inspiration every time.

Unfortunately, we quickly hit a bump in the road regarding our home study. After making several phone calls and leaving messages with our social worker, she finally called me back.

"I'm sorry, but I cannot complete the rest of your home study. I am not qualified to perform a home study for Colombia."

Oh, no! We knew this set us back quite a bit, yet we didn't know how much.

So naive at the time, I didn't have a clue how to find a social worker qualified to do a home study for Colombia. Another school year already started, severely limiting my time to do research and make phone calls during business hours. I hated to think of my children waiting any longer on us than necessary. I considered finding out who did the majority of the home studies in Austin for the families adopting the other Colombian children who came in the summer. Could she come to Dallas?

The program coordinator in the Austin area gave me a name to contact, so I sent a message to that social worker, who, of course, happened to be out of the office for a week. I reluctantly waited. What else could I do? Desperate to find somebody quickly in my own limited time, I neglected to research any other options. In the meantime, we spent a week filling out financial aid paperwork, applying for grants, and collecting letters of reference from our pastor, family, and friends.

Fortunately, the social worker responded to my e-mail quickly once she returned to her office. She could travel to Dallas to complete our home study, with fees reflecting her added travel expenses. She sent me the application (along with a list of all the required documents). Yep, we started completely over with the home study process.

So much for thinking we were ahead of the game. Now, we might even lag behind, plus we'd lost an entire month. Since our previous social worker had some of the information needed for our new home study, we requested her to send our entire packet back to us so we could forward most of it on to our new social worker. Thankfully, she complied quickly and refunded us the percentage of our fees to her that we didn't use for services so far. Since we'd already completed one out of the three visits, we couldn't get a full refund. However, the remaining amount covered the new fees.

We finally switched from one home study agency to the other, now working with both an adoption agency and a social worker who dealt specifically with these Colombian adoptions. I did feel a little uncomfortable, completely pulling out of a solid Christian agency to start up with two secular agencies. Suddenly, our Christ-connection we shared with the previous agency and social worker no longer existed. Now they saw us as people with a "religion" we lived by, with a "faith" not always understood. I hoped that wouldn't matter, as long as we got our kids. But honestly, it did matter, and it made the road ahead much more difficult and uncomfortable.

Our first agency prayed over our family. They prayed weekly over every family adopting a child through their organization. We took comfort in that. With our new agencies, nothing of the sort took place. Fortunately, our church family fulfilled that role and prayed us through the months ahead as we trudged through this overwhelming process.

Those first few steps consumed a great deal of time as we hurried to complete and send out all the applications and forms. After that, time crept by. I prayed for those children every single day. Their pictures motivated me and kept my heart filled with joy as I waited through each part of the process.

We couldn't schedule our home study for almost two whole months. Fortunately, this agency only required one visit. The social worker met with us as a family, as a couple, and then individually. We felt at ease talking with her. She walked through the house and mentioned a few areas needing attention, like a lock on the shed door. She seemed pleased and said she'd send us a copy of her report to go over before turning it in.

Then the next blow came.

"I will send you a complete rough draft within about four to eight weeks." The wait might extend for possibly two more months. Ugh.

Our children seemed to drift further and further away. I wished I could explain to them why it took so long. However, they didn't really know about a possible adoption. Someone told them we would try, so they had their suspicions, at least Juan David did. Viviana's young age prevented her from really understanding.

While we waited, we chased more documents on each list, including several background checks, fingerprints, medical forms, pet vaccinations, family photos, pictures of our home, etc., plus we continued to seek financial aid.

Where did we start with so much to tackle?

First, we contacted the psychologist on staff in the Counseling Department at our church to ask him to conduct our psychological evaluations. Not knowing what to expect, we surprisingly felt quite at ease through the evaluation. He also addressed the specific family history issues that Colombia requested, so everything seemed to go well.

He sent us home with a test, similar to a personality test, to complete separate from each other. It's one of those tests where you choose the first thing that comes to your mind. Trying to analyze your answers can actually skew the results or will not give an accurate description of your true personality. We both completed them on our own time and returned them to the psychologist to include the results with his report.

Our agency's guidelines stated to take a specific test, or "one similar" that showed a certain type of result. It looked for any psycho-social issues. Our psychologist went with the similar test because he always used it for these types of purposes, so we didn't think anything of it. We had no idea how much weight Colombia put on these test results.

I rejoiced every time I crossed a task off one of the many lists. Every accomplishment moved us closer to the day I could bring my children home. This lifelong dream became more of a reality each day. It humbled us to know God chose these two specific children for our family all along.

I wondered often how many ways God intertwined our lives since the day of their birth, preparing us for them and them for us. I journaled daily throughout it all, documenting every step we took, every penny we spent, and every time I thought about them. I wrote their story with passion, the story of God bringing our family together.

When time discouraged me, I tried to live by my new motto of faith. "It's all on God's timetable, and who am I to try to get ahead of his plan?" He knows the day we will travel to Colombia and the exact day they will officially become my children. (I desperately hoped for the spring, by Viviana's seventh birthday in April, also our tenth anniversary as a husband and wife. What a celebration!)

Despite all the "hurry-up and wait" instances, the tedious paperwork, and the added expenses, I still felt on top of the mountain. Nothing could give me more joy than pursuing this adoption. My children awaited me, and I would do everything necessary to bring them home. It amazed me to actually be in this process after dreaming for so many years. I reflected over many events in our lives and realized how God prepared and equipped us our entire lives for this purpose.

Humbling, to say the least.

GOD'S ENDLESS PROVISIONS

"He is faithful in all He does." Psalm 33:4b

Divine Calculations

So many appointments
and papers to track down,
so much of our income
going all over town.

What drove us to these measures
when we could just sit back?
Why go through all the trouble
when there are other things we lack?

Yet every penny spent
gives me an overwhelming joy,
to know that God provided it
all for an orphan girl and boy.

I gaze upon their picture
every morning as I pray.
I'm overwhelmed with gratitude
at how he's paved the way.

Sure, there have been some struggles,
surprising curves along our road,
but with our Divine compass,
the right direction always showed.

We haven't lacked a penny
to complete this paper chase.
We've never lacked direction
to make it through this maze.

God has given me such confidence,
knowing it's his timeline that counts.
he's provided all we've needed,
so who am I to have my doubts?

I know he brought these children
so clearly to our path.
It's all a matter of faith,
letting God do all the math.

"The hospital settled for less, and the difference between the two amounts covers our home study fees exactly!" Mike and I just stared at the numbers on the paper, in awe of God's calculations.

After living through financial disaster years earlier in our marriage, including bills from two surgeries with no insurance coverage, fears about money issues consumed me. We lived through days without money to pay the bills or even buy groceries. We couldn't even afford to keep a phone in our home, and we had to pick and choose what to pay each month. Creditors constantly contacted us, and my self-worth fell extremely low. I couldn't even fathom a day where we could financially pursue something like an adoption.

Thankfully, our God is faithful. He allowed us to suffer for a while to learn a few valuable lessons. Then, in his perfect time, he rescued us from the pit and set us on solid ground again. Several years later, when we felt the call to commit to the El Salvador adoption, we finally climbed our way back out of all past debt. When we obey his leading and follow, when we step into the waters, he parts them and provides a way. His time arrived for our children to join us, and he would provide the necessary resources to complete this adoption.

So I shouldn't have been surprised when each time we wrote a check, paid a fee, swallowed the expenses for an evaluation, paid extremely high postage for overnight mail to and from, paid for gas to drive four hours to apostille our documents (and then drive four hours back), etc., I never found a shortage of money in our account. It reminded me of the widow in the Bible whose flour and oil never ran out (I Kings 7:7-16). Not a single instance existed where we didn't have the money we needed in time for the next step. Nor did we find ourselves in need. We walked each step by faith. God never let us down.

God's constant faithfulness reminded us we chose the right path. We faced a financial monster. Yet now, face to face with the monster, God trumped our fear. I will never minimize the incredible ordeal involved in an international adoption process. I now have the utmost respect for anyone who has gone through it in order to bring home their child. But God used the experience in countless ways to show me his greatness in comparison to the fears I face. He strengthened my faith, and he grew in me a patience I didn't know I could possess, a patience I desperately needed for the road ahead.

Finally, after several months and various trials, we had a complete home study and psychological evaluation in hand. We liked the way the social worker portrayed us as a Christ-centered couple (which I did not expect, coming from a secular agency). We did not see any areas of concern in her report. Our psychologist pleased us by the way he described us, carefully showing how we overcame family history issues and allowed past struggles to help us find our way as a couple and a family with David.

The results of the personality assessment, however, did not settle so well with us. They pointed out the good, the bad, and the ugly. They suggested behaviors that can appear common among certain personality types, such as drugs and alcohol, manipulation, low self-esteem, insecurity, etc. I read through it several times before I understood it said we may show some of those tendencies due to our personality types. But if we did, it would likely be reflected either in the psychologist's findings or the social worker's. Once I realized that, I felt better because neither our psychologist nor our social worker portrayed us in any sort of negative light in their reports. That "realization," unfortunately, would come back to haunt me later.

Once the social worker finished her final report, she turned it in to the agency to put the official seal on it. However, the lady from that agency then e-mailed me with her own concerns after she read through the report herself.

"The financial information you provided only answered the basic questions. Due to your financial history as a couple, I need you to give me a detailed budget of your living expenses to prove your ability to take care of the special needs of two more children. Don't forget, they will need new clothes, shoes, and other accessories as soon as they come home."

My heart sank. If they worried about our financial status, why couldn't they bring that up in the beginning rather than wait till now? But, as we sat down to look at all of our expenses in detail, it actually helped us to take a good look at the physical, psychological, and financial needs of older adopted children.

We made room in the budget for not only their basic needs but also their mental and emotional needs. We found exact numbers for the cost of counseling, the cost of a special activity for each child to help them fulfill an emotional desire, and we still accounted for the cost of food, clothing, shoes, etc. Once again, God proved faithful and showed us ways to live frugally enough so the numbers would work out on paper. We received approval shortly after completing it.

Finally official, the state of Texas qualified and approved us to adopt up to two children from Colombia. Six whole months already passed since we met them. Once again, we felt like we stood on a mountaintop!

Now we could move on to the immigration stage. Once we received our official home study report in the mail, we could set up our appointment to get fingerprinted on this new level. It included another hefty fee of more than eight hundred dollars. These prints passed through the immigration stage to approve us to adopt a child from another country. This part could take months of waiting, the last step on the US side of the process before sending the completed paperwork (dossier) to Colombia for approval. It amazed me how many levels you had to be approved on, another reminder of our complete naivety when we began.

BEGINNING TO BOND

"And my God will meet all your needs according
to his glorious riches in Christ Jesus."
Philippians 4:19

Silence Broken

From the moment I first saw them
amidst the whole group of fourteen,
my heart embraced the siblings
I found on my computer screen.

After many prayers for guidance,
and a chance to spend a day with them,
I found my heart completely captured,
treasuring each moment like a gem.

Thus began a mound of paperwork,
an intense interrogation of our lives.
Each success and failure under a microscope
while we shared our passions and our drives.

Every day that I heard nothing,
I wondered what was wrong.
I fought between faith and anxiety,
knowing this process would be long.

Many days I'm filled with hope,
so humbled by such a call.
Other days I can't seem to rest,
so afraid of hitting a wall.

As I wait on yet another clearance,
and attempt to raise what funds remain,
I'm taking the opportunity
to hear their voices again.

We started with a simple phone call,
so brief yet so profound.
The silence has now been broken.
I don't want to miss a single sound.

I still can hear their voices,
our conversations play in my head.
I hear the background noise around them.
I remember every word they said.

He said he needed school supplies.
She said she had a lot of friends.
His environment seemed rather quiet,
Hers sounded loud and quite intense.

He said he was reading.
She worked on homework at the time.
He seemed polite and respectful.
Her telephone skills weren't so prime.

She said she was in first grade.
He said he was in grade four.
She talked about a doll and a suitcase.
He said I could call him more.

So now I don't have to wait
to start building the bond I so desire.
What a memory to pass on to my children
Of God bonding us over a wire . . .

Almost seven months passed since meeting our children. We hit many bumps in the road, completed more paperwork and cleared ourselves through more background checks than we ever imagined. Nothing went as planned or according to the timeline I originally assumed based on others' stories.

Some days I felt a sudden burst of inspiration and pressed on confidently. God led us this far already. He wouldn't let us or those precious children down.

Then other days I ran head on into a wall of anxiety, wondering if, after all of this, something could go wrong. When would we finally reach the end so we could travel to Colombia to get them? If we couldn't go in the summer time, a whole other dimension of details needed to work out because of school.

My pretty little picture didn't look so pretty anymore. I envisioned a beautiful puzzle where nearly every piece fit perfectly, but the remaining missing pieces left a gaping hole in the picture. What did our final masterpiece look like? What parts of our journey to our children had we not yet seen?

My heart ached for what Juan David and Viviana might be experiencing on their end. Did they think we changed our minds?

Did they wonder if a family might not ever come for them? Did they even still remember us, after having only spent two afternoons with us, now seven months ago? I assumed a multitude of questions consumed them after these seven months of complete silence on our end.

Through a random conversation with the kids' host family, I soon found out I could make phone calls to the kids during the process! The hosting program strives to keep them connected to a family or a caring adult after they leave. The continued communication helps solidify a bond, especially for an older child, before they ever join a family.

I contacted the program coordinator as soon as I found out! She couldn't believe I didn't know earlier or that these kids lost all contact with us when they returned home. She immediately made connections for me to find out what days and times the orphanage gave permission for the kids to receive phone calls. It thrilled me to know I could soon talk with them, hear their voices, and learn more about them while I continued to wait.

Their defender and their social worker both suggested I ask the kids questions about their daily life, their likes and dislikes, etc. I could let them know we were in the process of trying to adopt them, but I should not discuss the process with them in any way. Children in these circumstances struggle to handle the anxiety of waiting for such a possibility, wondering daily how much longer it might take.

I felt anxious and nervous as I dialed the number to the orphanage. I didn't even know what I would say, other than to ask if they still remembered me.

"Yes, I remember you. You're David's mom." That first phone call with Juan David felt so awkward, but I loved how he remembered David. Once I knew he remembered us, I asked question after question about his daily life. We talked comfortably with one another.

"I'm doing homework right now. . . . I still need school supplies. . . . I am in fourth grade. . . . I like math, and I love P.E. because I get to play soccer. . . . Yes, I would like for you to call me more." We only talked for a short while before I ran out of things to say.

"Hola, Tía!" Viviana could barely contain her excitement over getting a phone call! She called me Tía (Auntie), which sounded so sweet to me. She told me all about a doll she left in Texas and a suitcase the orphanage kept after she returned home. I heard a ton of noise in the background, and she definitely struggled with phone etiquette. I don't think she held the phone correctly because everything sounded muffled. I struggled to understand her words. I still cherished every moment of the conversation, taking in every single sound. I learned about her by listening to her environment. Priceless.

What a privilege to finally hear their voices again so much earlier than I thought.

With their sweet voices playing over and over in my head, I trudged through the paper chase with renewed enthusiasm. Their host family sent me a total of one hundred sixteen pictures of their summer adventures. I printed many of them and put them up all over the house. Now I had both a visual and an audio reminder of the purposes behind all this paperwork.

But I wanted to know more about their specific location while I talked with them. I looked up the name of their orphanage online, and I found much more than I expected, including lots of pictures and even some videos. Their living conditions actually impressed me. The orphanage appeared bright, clean, and child-friendly.

A huge surprise blessing soon overwhelmed me when I found a video posted online by a couple who adopted two children from the same orphanage. I got to see the outside of the buildings, the street where they lived, and I even found Viviana in the video! I couldn't mistake her sweet, high-pitched voice. That twenty second video lit up my world!

There she stood, my daughter, though much younger at the time. I can't even count the number of times I replayed that video, longing for the day I could hear that sweet voice in my home every single day.

The orphanage permitted me to call the kids two times a week at specific times in the evening. I always tried, but I didn't always reach them. My conversations with Viviana remained muffled, but sweet. I learned about her favorite colors, her interest and ability level in school, and whether or not she could read yet. She sure loved and missed the family who hosted her and her brother here in Texas.

Living with a family made a huge impression on her heart, a life-changing experience she would never forget. She adored their dog (and all animals in general). She seemed clueless about the adoption, so we purposely left it that way. My phone calls delighted her, and she continued to call me Tía. We kept the conversation topics pretty basic, but I did tell her I planned to visit her.

"I hope to go to Colombia to visit you someday so that I can see you again." That excited her and gave us a more solid purpose for our talks.

I couldn't reach Juan David as often, but our conversations took on a natural tone whenever we talked. I quickly found out he did know about our intent to adopt them.

"What do you think about that?" I asked hesitantly.

"It would be great!" Suddenly his voice filled with excitement, and his entire mood changed. He seemed so much more enthusiastic to talk and get to know me.

I wished Mike and David had more Spanish skills so they could talk to him, too. The more I learned about him confirmed what a great match he made for David as a brother. They both loved math, and Juan David said he loved P.E. because he could play soccer. Funny, David claimed recess as his favorite "subject" because he gets to play soccer. These two boys would make a great pair.

Being able to talk with my children perked me up again and helped me stay focused through the final steps of our adoption process. We wouldn't make it by April, as hoped, and it looked like we couldn't even make it by June.

God knew exactly what I needed at that point in time. Our paperwork finally arrived at the immigration level for processing. Up to ninety days might pass before receiving approval, but at least that gave us a number and time frame to go by. It helped to know things moved along, not as quickly as I preferred, but at least nothing stood at a standstill.

We still waited to hear if we'd qualified for any grants or financial aid to help us pay for the rest of the process. We watched God miraculously provide every penny so far. We still owed the final amount to our agency, roughly another five thousand dollars. That included the second half of their normal fee, a translation fee, and our attorney fee.

Around the same time, I found myself wrestling with God over a matter he pressed on my heart. I knew he asked me to give a little over three hundred dollars to someone in particular. I whined and complained, saying, "But God, I'm in the middle of trying to adopt two children. I could really use that money for this process."

He wouldn't take the burden off my heart, though. I already paid the bills for the month, subtracted the amount from our checking account and budgeted for the month without that money. I stalled on actually writing the check, but eventually I obeyed the still, small voice and wrote it. I felt the burden lift as I addressed the envelope and put it in the mail.

God taught me an incredible lesson that day. He couldn't show me until I obeyed. You see, I put that check in the mailbox first thing in the morning before I left for work. That evening, Mike brought in the new mail, and we went through it together.

While I read one piece of mail and he another, Mike suddenly shouted out, "Rachelle! Listen to this!"

He proceeded to read the letter in his hand, saying a check for five thousand dollars had been sent to our agency to help cover our expenses. I wanted to cry. I felt so elated, yet ashamed at the same time. I'd argued with God over a measly three hundred dollars, and he turned around and blessed us with the entire remaining amount owed to our agency. Where God guides, he also provides, always.

Yet the blessings didn't stop there. That same weekend, a couple in our church offered us an entire girl's bedroom set they didn't need any more.

"Thank you, Father. Thank you. Your goodness is so humbling."

We really grew as a family during those last few months of waiting on our final document, our immigration approval. My weekly phone calls to Juan David and Viviana made their role in our lives a reality.

"Is David there? Is your husband home? Pass the phone to them, please." Viviana loved hearing Mike and David's voices on the phone, even if they didn't understand more than a few words she said.

"How did David's team do in their last game? Did they win?" Juan David asked about David's soccer games almost every time I called, connecting them more as brothers.

These kids were real, no longer just pictures of two faces we'd met months ago and nearly forgotten about. Our bond with them grew day by day.

David talked about them as his brother and sister, and we talked about them as our children. They say once you adopt, you love the child as if they had always been your child. So why not love them and talk of them that way from the beginning? It made sense. We already claimed them as part of our family, a part of each one of us. I even noticed in my phone calls with Juan David that he already thought of David as his own little brother, too. We never talked about the adoption or where we stood in the process, but he knew, and to him, we already made a family of five.

The adventure of watching God continue to provide for our every need (not just financially) helped make the wait time much more bearable. We found out another Christian organization awarded us a Matching Grant for twenty-five hundred dollars, meaning another possible five thousand dollars toward our travel expenses within Colombia if enough friends and family donated to match it.

We held three garage sales over the next month to raise money for the airline tickets. So many people donated to our sales, helping us raise over a thousand dollars, possibly enough to cover both kids' plane tickets to come home. Everything seemed to fall right into place as we neared the end of our journey.

Still needing to make another trip to Austin to apostille a few documents, we planned to at least stop by our friends' house while there (the ones who opened their home to us the two weekends we traveled to meet Juan David and Viviana). They ended up having to travel out of town that weekend, but they arranged for a neighbor to meet us to send us home with a beautiful bunk bed set for Juan David and David's room that their own boys already outgrew.

"Thank you, God."

Now, he not only provided the bedroom set for Viviana's room, but he also provided the bunk beds for David and Juan David to share. Endless provisions continued coming! What a beautiful experience for our family.

Our faith grew exponentially. God brought everything together, showing us his plans are not our plans, but they are always better. His timing is not our timing, but it's always perfect.

Juan David asked me to send him a special blanket he left behind in Austin, a blue quilt someone made for him. On our most recent trip to Austin, his host family happened to send us back with all of the kids' toys, clothes, and belongings that they purposely held onto for their adoptive family. Special items they knew the kids would love to see again in their new home, including the blankets made for them!

I couldn't wait to tell Juan David I finally held his blanket in my possession. We set up the bunk beds as soon as we got home, and I draped his blanket over the railing on the top bunk. It felt like I brought a little part of him home, too. Seeing it on the bed where he would one day sleep made him feel so much closer. Still, my heart ached for him more every day. Eight months now slipped through our fingers.

With everything falling into place, I knew our time must be

near. Then, much to our dismay, we hit another road block, a pretty big one, actually. After reviewing our paperwork on the immigration level, they now expressed concern over issues in our psychological evaluation. They considered not approving us without documentation of how we professionally resolved those issues.

What? You mean, we got this far, down to our final piece of documentation, and it could all end here? You're kidding me! Could my heart handle much more? Without this approval, we could not continue the process, thus losing our children.

This pending issue actually traced all the way back to the very beginning. They wanted a written letter from the counselor we saw years ago, the counselor we couldn't find. We went round and round with them to explain why we couldn't provide such a letter. Finally, our agency convinced them our psychologist could provide the information they wanted.

The psychologist wrote up an addendum to our first evaluation and sent it in. Still not pleased, the immigration officer brought up more unclear issues from the personality assessment over the phone with the psychologist—the personality test that suggested tendencies our specific personality types might lead to, like drugs and alcohol. He finally convinced the officer we showed no signs of such behaviors.

By the grace of God, the immigration officer finally approved us. With this last approval, we could finally send our entire mound of paperwork to Colombia.

"Thank you, Father. Satan may attack me and make me doubt, but you hold complete control. Forgive me for my unbelief."

From that moment on, I clung to my favorite verse, one I claimed as the theme of our journey. "Blessed is she who has believed that what the Lord has said to her will be accomplished" (Luke 1:45).

Nine solid months passed since we met our children. "I'm coming, my darlings, as soon as I can!"

We still needed to wait for the written immigration approval to arrive. Once we could send everything to Colombia, it usually took about four to eight weeks before receiving their national approval, the referral for your child, and a travel date.

Time moved much more quickly now! I could almost see the end in sight! Nearing the end of April, we began to draw another school year to a close. What a surprise when the staff at my elementary school showered me with the blessing of a money tree to help cover our needs when our children came home.

A teacher who knew me well and shared my faith in Christ wrote out several Bible verses on faith and tied them all over the tree. Long after we used up the money, I kept the verses tied to the tree, my faith tree. It touched my heart deeply.

I continued to call the orphanage every week, sometimes twice a week to each home, to talk to my children. Our bond grew stronger, and we felt more comfortable with one another every day. Viviana especially loved knowing I called them both.

"Will you call my brother tonight?" She asked me the same thing almost every time I called.

"Viviana, I haven't been able to talk to Juan David for the last two weeks. Did he get a new phone number or move to a different house?"

"Hmmm. Let me ask." She'd disappear for a minute or so, then she returned to the phone to read off some numbers to me. After getting a new number from her on three different occasions, I finally regained contact with him. He'd moved into a different house within the orphanage, so the number changed. I made sure to let him know I still tried to call every single week. I wondered if he thought I forgot about him.

"I need to go now. I love you, Sweetie."

"Okay, Tía. I love you, too." Her words brought joy to my heart.

I started to tell both kids I loved them before I hung up the phone. Juan David didn't quite know how to respond to that yet, but Viviana told me she loved me in return. I could almost hear the smile in her voice every time she said it. I think the time I spent calling just her over those few weeks I couldn't reach her brother actually helped me bond even more with her. I cherished every moment because I only got to talk to her. I didn't cut our conversations short in order to have time to call her brother, too.

"When are you coming to see me, Tía?" She still didn't know about our plans to adopt her, but she constantly asked when I could visit.

"Soon, Princess, soon," I replied, hopeful my words held truth.

LONGING FOR MY CHILDREN

We wait for you; your name and renown are the desire of our hearts. Isaiah 26:8b

Unexpected Tears
(To Viviana)

Thoughts of you dance through my head,
yet much to my surprise,
I find my heart aching
as the tears fall from my eyes.

This waiting has been equally hard
both for you and for me.
You long for me to come see you,
I wonder when "Adoption Day" will be.

An expectant mother often wonders
about the color of her baby's eyes.
I've already looked deeply into yours
and envision them with each sunrise.

A pregnant mother imagines
the sound of her child's voice.
I've memorized the sound of yours,
even amidst so much background noise.

I've heard your smile when you're happy,
I've heard you giggle with delight,
I've detected sadness in your voice,
and I've heard your weariness at night.

You keep asking when I'm coming,
I keep wondering when I'll go.
We both dream of reuniting,
as our bond continues to grow.

You don't forget a single word
that I utter to you over the phone.
I cherish every word you say
as I long to bring you home.

I expected to bond with your brother,
as our talks carry a more natural tone.
I expected to win your heart through his
due to how your love for him has shown.

Now every time I say I love you
and you say you love me, too,
a part of my heart lies broken
until the law declares it all true.

I ache for you, my Princess,
more than I ever thought I would.
My arms long to hold you
and call you "mi hija" for good.

To Walk in Your Shoes
(To Juan David)

Each day seems an eternity,
waiting for this process to go through.
As much as my heart aches,
I wonder what it's like for you.

You've known almost all along
that we'd come for you someday.
You said it excited you
that our plans were underway.

We diligently pressed on
while you and I talked casually over the phone.
How often have you wondered
when we'd bring you home?

Has your heart been torn between
your hope to come and longing to stay?
Do you even struggle
knowing you'll leave the orphanage some day?

They described you as a good kid,
a great attitude you had,
Respectful and obedient,
though not having a family made you sad.

What have you had to suffer?
What have you had to work through?
When did you last hear from your mother?
Will it be hard to call me Mom, too?

I'm longing to finally see you again
to help mend where your heart may be bruised,
to see things from your perspective,
to know what it's like to walk in your shoes.

My son, it's been a long road—
longer even for you than for me.
Keep holding on to your hopes
To soon be part of our family.

Another school year ended with so much added to our recent chapter of life experiences. I rejoiced that our paperwork finally made its way to Colombia. I also celebrated when I heard enough donations came in to match our twenty-five hundred dollar Matching Grant! A long, challenging year now ended with blessing and hope.

I left my classroom as ready as I could for the possibility of a substitute starting the following year for me in my absence in case I found myself in Colombia in August. I wrote seven full weeks of plans, including all the daily procedures I teach at the beginning of the year, but I still desperately hoped God might get us there and back before the following school year. Though highly unrealistic, I knew my God was able.

I grew closer to Viviana with every phone call I made to her. I treasured her voice, one of the sweetest sounds to my ear, and I couldn't imagine my life without hearing the sound of that voice eventually in my home. A curious little thing, she asked questions about anything and everything.

"What's your favorite color? Where do you work? Do you like your job? What are you wearing? What is David doing right now? Where are you?"

She wasn't content with knowing the what--she always probed further to find out the how's and the why's to everything.

I loved her more daily, and I suspected she grew to love me more and more, as well. She always wanted to hear Mike and David, too, and she squealed with delight every time she heard their voices, even if actual communication between them never went past the basic greeting.

We confidently assumed we would travel to Colombia sometime that summer to see our children again. With school out, I found an abundance of time to prepare our home for their arrival. Our extra bedroom currently served as an office in our house, with a fairly large desk, a built-in filing cabinet, the computer, and a closet full of Mike's work clothes. Now we needed to empty the room of its contents in order to repaint it and refill it with things for her.

With a little rearranging and moving things around within the house, an empty room and closet soon awaited all the preparations needed for the arrival of our Colombian princess. We set out to paint her room, and then we enthusiastically repainted the entire house to hopefully welcome both kids home soon.

After painting, I set to work on the décor in her bedroom. Viviana loved the color orange. That didn't surprise me, since it expressed her vibrant, bubbly personality. She asked for an orange blanket on one occasion, so we bought a reversible comforter for her bed with bright orange on one side and hot pink with orange stripes on the other side. Bright orange curtains soon hung from her window, and her outlet covers and light switch covers stood out on her walls with orange paint. We even found a cute little locker at a garage sale and painted it orange.

Our friends hadn't yet given us the furniture for her room yet, so we put a few rickety old dressers in there for the time being to collect clothing as we accumulated it. I found lots of sweet little toys, shoes, and outfits at various yard sales throughout the summer. I enjoyed every minute shopping for that little girl!

Her room lacked one final touch, the perfect decoration for the shelf on her far wall. I still owned my favorite keepsakes from my childhood, my collection of Cabbage Patch Kids. I had seven different dolls as a little girl, each one with a different "story" and personality, complete with a birth certificate and adoption papers. I took each one out of the box they'd sat in for years, cleaned them up a bit, and carefully placed them across the shelf. I displayed each one with their adoption papers.

I knew without a doubt she'd love those dolls, but how fitting we kept their official "adoption" paperwork. She would share something in common with all of her new dolls. Oh, I could hardly wait to bring her home! Her room cried out for her.

One evening when I called her, I caught her in one of those curious moods. "Where do you live? What is your house like? Tell me about every room in your house!"

We started with the front porch, my quiet, peaceful place where I sat to talk to her. Then I moved into the kitchen and described it to her, followed by the living room, the play room, my bedroom, David's bedroom and the extra room, which I couldn't really call an office anymore.

"Why do you have an extra room? What do you use it for?" Try explaining that concept to a little girl who lived in a house with twenty-six other girls.

I had to bite my tongue to keep from blurting out, "It's your room, Sweetheart! It's just waiting for you to get here."

Preparing for Juan David didn't require as much work since he and David would share a room. They liked the same things and would likely share many of them (bunk beds, soccer balls and equipment, toys and games). Plus we didn't want to do much pre-shopping for Juan David, already a pre-teen. We wanted to give him more of a choice in what we purchased for him. His top bunk awaited his arrival, we planned to put him on a soccer team right away, and half a closet full of donated clothes waited for him.

Juan David knew our plan to adopt him all along. We rarely ever discussed it, and I found it hard to not slip up and say something as the time got closer. Since Viviana knew I'd visit someday and bring her presents, I accidentally carried the same conversation over into one of my phone calls with him. He quickly closed up after he heard me say the word visit. I wondered if it made him think we'd changed our minds. He didn't want a visitor. He wanted a family.

I sensed his attitude from the start of our phone call relationship. He didn't mind talking, but he stayed pretty closed off until I mentioned being in the process to try to adopt him (specifically what they told me I could tell him). His whole mood changed after that, and he talked openly and freely, almost as if he needed a purpose for our conversations. He wasn't going to let just anybody in.

In our following conversation, we talked heart to heart, and I told him the truth. I knew deep down that I didn't make the wisest choice by having that conversation. On the other hand, knowing his age, I knew I needed to speak honestly with him. I needed him to know he could trust me. (I didn't consider how such a conversation might come back to haunt me later.)

Our phone calls felt more fun and lighthearted from that moment on, helping me convince myself I'd made the right choice. We compared information about our countries and cultures a lot.

"What month do you celebrate Valentine's Day in your country? What month do you start school? When does your school year end? What do you do at Halloween? Does David dress up? Do you wear a costume?" He loved learning about our holidays, our educational system, and about the way we do things here in the States. I enjoyed having him teach me all about his own culture in Colombia, too.

That summer held so many ups and downs. On one particular Sunday, our teaching pastor preached a special sermon on adoption. Our Adoption Ministry at the church set up a booth for anyone to find out more about the ministry after the service, plus to advertise an upcoming mini-conference later in the summer to help anyone learn how to start an adoption process. Mike and I volunteered at the booth at our campus for all three services. I couldn't think of a more wonderful way to use our waiting time than to encourage and inspire other couples to look into adoption, too.

During the service, the media team played a slideshow with pictures of many adoptive families in the church, as well as pictures of those in the process. Some couples held up a flag of the country they planned to adopt from and a big question mark.

For our picture, the three of us held up a picture of Juan David and Viviana, looking at them with a longing in our eyes. The slide show brought tears to my eyes every time I watched it. One day soon our family picture would indeed be complete. We would have more than a picture to hold—we'd have two children to hold in our arms and give hugs and kisses to every night.

After the final service, we met with some friends for lunch. I probably glowed for hours after such an inspiring morning. As we left the restaurant a little while later, we all spotted a truck in the adjacent parking lot with puppies for sale.

"Please, please, please, please, please can we go see them?" David begged, tugging on my arm. I'm not a dog person, but I complied. I'm still not sure how this happened, but one precious little pup completely captured my heart.

Still reflecting over the morning service, Viviana dominated my thoughts. She wanted a dog. She loved dogs. She even asked me to send her host family's dog to her in the mail because she loved it so much during her summer stay. She squealed every time she heard my neighbor's dog bark through the phone.

Before I knew it, I reached for the cash in my pocket and walked away with a dog.

"I can't believe we have a dog!" David repeated himself over and over into the evening.

Yeah, that made two of us.

However, that pup turned out to be the sweetest thing in the world. So sweet, we called her Sweetie. I took her outside on my porch without a leash, and she obediently sat there. We snapped tons of pictures and later invited David's cousins to come meet her. Even I fell completely in love with that little dog.

When I called Juan David and Viviana three days later, I told them about our newest addition to the family.

"What? You got a dog? What color is she? Is she big or small? Can I have her?" Viviana sounded like she might jump through the phone with so much excitement!

Once again, I had to restrain myself from saying, "It's your puppy, Sweetheart."

Much to our dismay our bliss did not last long. We entered into a season of grief a few days later. Our pup fell ill and passed away right before our eyes. Apparently she'd been exposed to parvo, a deadly puppy disease, shortly before we got her. We tried to nurse her back to health via the vet's instructions, but the disease took her fast.

From one Sunday to the next, we traveled from the top of the mountain to a valley of despair. We spent six short days loving our precious little puppy, and now we grieved losing her.

David took it hard. "Why did she have to die?"

I never helped him grieve before, and it broke my heart to see him hurt so badly. Then when I called Viviana a few days later and told her, she burst into tears and cried through our entire conversation. I never heard her cry before, and it, too, broke my heart. I wanted to kick myself for making such an impulsive purchase.

Summer pressed on, despite our loss, and we all grew restless. I focused my energy on spending quality time with David, cherishing our last summer as just the two of us. We rode bikes, played games every day, read books, ate ice cream together, and talked a bunch. It proved to be a good summer for us and for our relationship.

That summer held challenges, too. Juan David struggled with anxiety and began to misbehave in the orphanage, probably because he knew he likely wouldn't live there much longer. Mike and I stressed about work, not knowing how to plan for an indefinite leave of absence when we didn't even know when we could leave.

I finally accepted we'd likely travel during the following school year, so I searched for a qualified substitute to cover my class. For a long absence, I needed a certified bilingual teacher, definitely not an easy position to fill. I dreaded the task of making so many phone calls until I found one.

By the third call, I found someone interested, miraculously someone bilingual and certified to teach, and a Christian adoptive parent, too! Having walked a similar road to adoption, she understood my vague timeline, and she encouraged me and prayed for me! Once again, God came through, showing how far ahead of me he walks.

"Forgive me, Father, for my unbelief. How could I doubt you planned even this detail, as well?"

The month of July passed by slowly after that. Each time I called my agency for updated news, they gave me the same answer. "We haven't heard anything new, Rachelle. We're on Colombia's time now, so we need to wait patiently."

Sigh. That's not what I wanted to hear. What in the world made it take so long?

The date soon fell on July 20 again, Colombia's Independence Day. A solid year already passed since we'd met our children. We wanted to make the day special again, despite all of our frustrations. So, we headed back to Austin for an event scheduled with the new children that came from Colombia that year. They hosted another picnic at the same lake where we met Juan David and Viviana the year before.

God refreshed and renewed our spirits by letting us meet some wonderful people who understood the process of adopting from Colombia. A Christian couple who adopted their daughter two years prior gave us several travel tips to keep in mind. Another couple shared their story of adopting a girl right before her sixteenth birthday, which would have made her unadoptable internationally if the process had not been expedited.

We met two other families still in process to adopt children that came the summer before, just like us. We desperately needed these connections at this point in the game. Like a breath of fresh air, they perked us back up and kept us going. Seeing other families now complete reminded us it would all be worth it when we finally brought our children home.

I even met the chaperone who accompanied the kids from Colombia. She told me more about my kids' specific orphanage and living conditions. She thanked me for pursuing their adoption because very little possibility existed to find a family in their own country due to their ages. She assured me it shouldn't take much longer. She even offered to deliver a letter to Juan David and Viviana for me!

We returned to Austin again the following weekend for another activity. I gave the chaperone two letters to take back for Juan David and Viviana. We breathed in more encouragement from the new families we met the week before, plus God allowed us to meet even more people. We didn't feel so alone anymore as we waited for "the call."

AN ANSWER WE DIDN'T EXPECT

"My soul is weary with sorrow; strengthen me
according to your word."
Psalm 119:28

The Call

So long I have waited
to finally get the call,
built up such anticipation
after climbing many a wall.

We saw our God move mountains,
we watched him part the sea.
We saw money fall from Heaven
for this adoption to really be.

God's fingerprints were evident
As he opened wide the door,
We never lacked a penny
And were even blessed with more.

So many rallied around us,
and carried us in prayer,
We didn't foresee this path,
yet we knew God led us there.

Today when I saw who called,
My heart completely skipped a beat.
Was this the call we awaited?
I could barely stay in my seat!

I never could have imagined
what I was about to be told.
Our petition to adopt denied,
The words still seem so cold.

After all of the hurdles we jumped,
after passing each approval we sought,
after giving our lives to these children,
I never felt so distraught.

Could we send more information?
Could we visit them like we'd said?
Is there any way to appeal this?
Now what lies ahead?

I'm overwhelmed with confusion.
Do I grieve or do I fight?
I sit here speechless, in utter shock,
Wishing this dark tunnel had more light.

It came. After an entire summer of waiting and wondering what took so long, the call finally came. I recognized the Adoption Agency's number immediately on my caller ID when I heard the first ring. My heart spun in circles.

Could it be that long-awaited phone call to tell me they approved us, allowing us to soon reunite with our precious children in Colombia? I don't know if I've ever felt such anticipation upon answering a phone, but nothing prepared me to hear the words expressed on the other end of the phone line that day.

"Colombia asked that the adoption not go through."

Wh-wh-what did she say? The words hit me like a brick, stunning me, leaving me speechless for a minute. I didn't know how to respond. I didn't know what to say.

Am I having a bad dream, a nightmare I could still wake up from? This couldn't be happening. Not after all that . . . not after everything that God . . . not after he clearly gave these children to us and worked out every last detail of the process.

This just couldn't be. They made a mistake and called the wrong person. My children, my sweet Juan David and Viviana, had waited for us for so long. They were coming home soon! I'd never been so sure of anything in my entire life. God always meant for them to join our family. I loved them. We loved them, and they loved us in return.

I had to do something. I had to fix this, to make it right. Who could I talk to that would hear me out? I had to stop this absurdity.

The rest of the phone call remains a blur to me, as well as the following hours, days, and weeks. I remember I didn't sleep that night. I spent the entire night on my knees in tears, crying my heart out to the God who created me, the God who gave me those children. I prayed scripture after scripture as the night passed.

Mike and David somehow slept, but I couldn't. Beside myself with grief, I felt so determined to fix whatever fell apart in this process. I had to find a way to still make it work, to point out a huge misconception somewhere. I fully convinced myself it would not end this way.

Our agency's director called to personally break the news to us even before she received an official translation from Colombia to send to me. She read bits and pieces of the letter over the phone, specific comments explaining the denial of our petition.

The letter made such inaccurate claims I couldn't even begin to understand. We were too withdrawn and introverted. Mike struggles to form close relationships. David felt nervous about sharing a room. I was self-conscious and unable to be assertive. We had misconceived ideas about adoption. We obviously didn't have a close bond with our son and did not prepare him well enough for adoptive siblings.

Where did all of this information come from? Didn't the reports from our social worker and psychologist prove these descriptions wrong? What made us look so withdrawn and introverted? We travel on mission trips all the time, living day in and out with people from all walks of life, building lifelong relationships with those who travel with us. What about all of our church involvement in life groups, growth groups, the adoption ministry group, etc. Those comments played over and over in my head. I didn't understand.

How could the letter say we didn't have a close bond with our son or prepare him well enough for his adoptive siblings? We thought an adoption like this actually prepared David more because we already knew the children we attempted to adopt. We included them in our daily life from the beginning, through pictures, purchases, phone calls, prayers, and conversation. We prayed for them, talked with and about them, dreamed about them, anticipated their arrival, prepared for them, etc.

We constantly talked with David to address his concerns, fears, and excitement. We both shared an incredible bond with him and did nothing but prepare him on a daily basis for the arrival of two new siblings and all of the changes they might bring to our family.

Of course he felt anxious to share his room! He never shared it before, but he also longed for the day his brother would sleep on the top bunk of his bed, keeping him company in his room. Once

Juan David's things accumulated on his shelves and in his closet, the two boys, in actuality, already began to share his bedroom. He had mixed emotions I assumed were normal. I never imagined the negative light those emotions could shadow over our case.

The comment in the letter about our misconceptions about adoption remained a mystery to me. I guess everybody has their own misconceptions they have to work through, but until I could read that formal letter of denial from Colombia, I felt baffled.

All the other "stuff" mentioned came straight from that personality assessment, the one that gave a "true picture" of our personality types and the tendencies they could lead to. Whoever read through it took it all out of context. How could I prove that? Someone completely misread us on a piece of paper. We had to appeal this, to go down there to meet them in person. Then they could determine if we fit those descriptions or not.

Those children counted on us. How could we possibly let them down? God wouldn't do that to them. Would he?

After a weekend of tears and prayer, we felt a sense of peace to appeal this decision. God walked with us. He brought us this far and brought Juan David and Viviana this close to having a family again. Satan worked here, once again attacking us, stealing our joy, trying to destroy our family and our faith.

By the time we talked with our agency's director again, we had a plan ready to set in motion. I must admit she seemed helpless at this point and did not communicate well with us. I will always have suspicions that our own agency let us down in some way, but I also possessed a strong enough faith to know God was bigger than an agency.

This situation held a purpose. He allowed it to happen, even if we didn't understand why. We claimed confidence over a happy ending, one bringing him even more glory than completing the adoption in the timing we hoped.

With another new school year ready to begin, I found myself bombarded with adoption paper work all over again. To start, we wrote an appeal, a four-page letter in Spanish explaining ourselves, also pointing out at least one mistranslation we knew about. We poured out our hearts, restating our firm commitment to these two children.

One of my bilingual teammates proofread and edited the letter for me, and then a Colombian coworker looked over it again after that. We also gathered more documentation, including a rebuttal letter from our psychologist and a new letter from our social worker restating her complete approval of us. We requested letters from family and close friends, as well, who could prove our sociability in contrast to the socially withdrawn people described in that denial letter. Our agency agreed to attach a letter, too.

I finally received the official letter from Colombia, so I immediately glanced at the Spanish letter, not the translation my agency sent with it. I wanted to read how the person stated all those comments in Spanish. Then I compared translations.

One particular sentence in the letter stated that I feared Juan David would likely wander the streets in search of food. What? I never said that! Why in the world would I ever say such a thing? Where did that come from? Of course they thought I had misconceived ideas about adoptive children if they thought I said something crazy like that! Something must have gone terribly wrong in the translation of our documents.

I scanned through our copy of the psychological evaluation looking for anything written even close to such an idea. In the paragraph addressing our fears of adoption, our psychologist quoted our agreement over the challenge of raising a teenager. Our realm of parenting experience only prepared us for a seven-year-old. We'd always been careful about what we exposed our seven-year-old to or gave him the freedom to do, still not even allowing him to cross a street without holding someone's hand. Juan David, on the other hand, roamed the streets alone as a child before the orphanage took him in. Those streets exposed him to things our own son didn't even know existed.

We took the risk of bringing Juan David's history into our home with great faith. Even so, we verbally acknowledged the risk.

So our psychologist quoted me saying, "He's likely to be more 'streetwise' than our biological son."

I don't know if I chose the best word to use in that conversation, but I knew the context and our psychologist understood. However, the person who translated the documents obviously didn't understand that context because that's where he said I believed Juan David would likely search the streets for his food. Our appeal would certainly address the fact that we felt, or better yet, knew, errors existed in the translation.

When I talked with our psychologist, he couldn't believe everything stated in that denial letter! He assured me none of it reflected what he personally said about us. As he read the letter, he shook his head, saying, "Wow. This is like a slap in the face. They took everything I said completely out of context."

He willingly wrote a new letter, rebutting the statements made against us and restating his approval of us. He chose his words even more carefully this time due to the translation factor.

The only statement in the denial that came from our home study regarded our son's nervousness to share his room. Our social worker wrote a new letter for us, once again giving her approval of us. She described all the steps we'd taken to prepare our son for the arrival of his new siblings as a way to address his concern over sharing a room.

My faith and hope built up again. I knew we could prove every single statement in that denial letter as inaccurate or misinterpreted information. While preparing our appeal, letters from family and friends poured in. Along with letters from our psychologist and social worker, our appeal now contained multiple personal letters stating beautiful things about our family.

In the meantime, I didn't know how to proceed with my phone calls to the kids and the relationship I built with them over the last six months. I sent an e-mail to the person in Colombia who arranged for them to participate in the summer hosting program in the States. I explained the situation, saying we would send an appeal soon because we felt they made their decision based on a mistranslation. I asked her if I should still stay in contact with the kids.

"I'm so sorry to hear about this. Since you plan to appeal the decision, I feel it very important, for the kids' sake, for you to maintain contact with them. I hope everything turns out well for all of you." She responded quickly with a positive tone in her message.

I didn't call them at all over the last two weeks, but the kids still heard from me! The summer chaperone returned to Colombia and delivered my letters to them sometime during those two weeks of silence. My letters expressed how much we loved them, missed them, and prayed for them. I tucked a picture of our kitties in Viviana's letter, and I sent Juan David a picture of David. I'd never sent them anything before due to the cost. By the time I finally called again, they both seemed ecstatic to hear my voice and thanked me repeatedly for sending them letters.

Wow. My heart melted. I didn't explain why I hadn't called for a while, obviously, and I realized through our conversations they didn't know anything had happened. Viviana kept me on the phone for at least forty minutes, not accepting a single excuse for needing to let her go earlier. I heard live music in the background. I recognized it as a Christian song I learned either in Argentina or in one of the many Spanish churches I'd attended over the years, but I couldn't place it. "It's a song about God, like you told me!"

Wow, again. My letter expressed how much God loved her and how much I prayed for her, and now I saw the impression my words made on her heart. The person in the background began praying, and she joined in at certain points in the prayer. I considered this one of the most special phone calls I'd ever made to that little girl. God let me know he held her and took care of her for me.

I called Juan David that evening, too, and he suddenly wanted my e-mail address and gave me his. Apparently his house parent bought a computer, meaning we might have a chance to finally communicate via e-mail, as well.

It took forever for us to exchange e-mail addresses that night.

We kept mistaking almost every other letter, but eventually we got them straight. Not only had I not lost contact with the kids yet, but now I might have even more chances to communicate with Juan David. Yes, God still worked. He hadn't finished our story yet. I could not even imagine how God planned to use our e-mail address exchange that night.

Almost ready to send our complete appeal now, our agency's director gave me permission to contact another family who'd successfully appealed a denial in the past. The summer hosting program only knew of two past denials. Both families traveled to Colombia to appeal, only one went home with a child. We had a fifty-fifty chance.

After talking with the family, I felt a renewed sense of hope. "Yes, your situation seems similar to our experience. They didn't like several things they read in our psychological evaluation either. I would not accept their denial, though. I just couldn't. Once the committee met us in person, they realized we were good people, very committed to the adoption. They let us keep our daughter in our custody for the full seven weeks we stayed in Colombia to then complete the adoption. Don't worry. I think your situation will turn out fine, as well."

However, they didn't go through near as much trouble to build and present their appeal. They said their caseworker simply requested a date for them to meet with the committee and had them collect a few extra documents. They didn't authenticate anything, nor did they even mail anything to Colombia. They took the documents with them in hand only a few short weeks later.

Ugh! If we used the same agency, why did the director tell me to collect and authenticate all this stuff to send first before even requesting a date for us to go down there? The next morning, I called the director to ask her myself.

"Well, I think it might give you a better chance if the committee can look over everything before they meet you. Once we send it all to Colombia, I will arrange a date for you to go." I'll always wonder if putting more energy into trying to get down there rather than in sending more papers would have led to a different outcome.

In fact, our agency really floundered once we had everything ready to put in the mail. "Send it all straight to Colombia to the Head of Adoptions."

A few hours later, "No, we think it's better to send it to our agency representative in Colombia so she can look it over and then advocate better for you."

Yet still within the same day, "Wait. Send it all to us first so we can add a cover letter and send it to Colombia for you. It will get more priority coming directly from an agency."

We sent everything straight to her the following day.

Appeal sent. Now we waited. And waited. And waited.

Nothing.

"Tía, when will you visit me? Will you bring me presents? Can you bring me sunglasses? Can you buy me an orange blanket? I love you, Tía. I miss you."

My bond continued to grow and even deepen with the kids. Neither one let me off the phone without telling me first how much they loved me. We'd come a long way with both of them. Juan David tried his best to demonstrate patience, but I could tell his heart hurt as he wondered why it took so long. Viviana could hardly wait for me to visit. I already packed a suitcase full of clothes and toys she'd asked me to bring her.

However, God, being God, constantly gave me reminders of his sovereignty and his presence in my life. A new little girl joined my second grade bilingual class at school. While talking with her at recess one day, she told me she used to live in Colombia! In fact, her older sister still resided there.

My students come from all over, but the majority of them usually come from Mexico and a maybe a few from Central America (usually El Salvador and sometimes Honduras). Never do they come all the way from South America. Luck didn't bring the first Colombian student directly to my class. God did that.

My heart latched on to that little Colombian girl immediately. God gave her to me to love, guide, and nurture until I could bring my own little Colombian girl home. I even imagined her and Viviana's friendship when she arrived later in the year. Wouldn't it be precious to have two little Colombian girls in the same grade?

My phone calls with Viviana grew longer each week. No matter how many times I told her I needed to go, she would quickly say, "Wait!" Then she thought of something else to tell me or ask me. I even missed out on calling Juan David several times because she kept me on the phone too long. The orphanage maintained a strict calling schedule.

Juan David's newest request completely surprised me. "Will you call me this Saturday afternoon at 2:00 when I'm at Viviana's house? I asked for permission for you to call while we are together. My older brother, Julian, will spend the afternoon there, too, and he really wants to meet you."

"I will try." The thought of calling at a different time made me nervous, so I couldn't promise Viviana's house parent would actually let me talk to them.

Saturday came, and I nervously picked up the phone to call Viviana's house at precisely two o'clock. One of her house parents reprimanded me once in the past for calling at the wrong time. I hated to do anything to jeopardize her trust in me. I wanted and needed her support more than anything. However, Juan David assured me I already had their permission.

I asked for Viviana, and they passed the phone right to her.

"Tía!" She squealed when she heard my voice, especially on a Saturday. I asked about Juan David, and she eagerly passed the phone to him. He said hello and almost immediately passed the phone to Julian.

"When are you coming for my brother and sister?" Wow. What could I say?

"The process is complicated, but we're trying to keep things moving as quickly as we can." I don't remember anything else we might have said to each other that day, but I'll never forget hearing his voice for the first time.

His voice sounded similar to Juan David's voice, but definitely older. We held a short conversation before he passed the phone back to Juan David. He and Viviana passed the phone back and forth a few times before they needed to go. I loved connecting with them together to witness more of their brother-sister relationship.

It couldn't be much longer now. Our relationship felt more real every day. God allowed too many things to progress. I could not even fathom him tearing it apart. He must have allowed me to grow even closer to them for a reason.

Now September, things got tense as our whole life hung in the air. Mike saved his vacation for the entire year in order to take as much time as possible to stay in Colombia with me to complete the adoption. His year started over again in late September, meaning he'd lose the vacation he never used from the previous year.

I relayed the situation to my agency's director. "Is there any way you can request for us to appeal in person specifically within the next two weeks due to our job circumstances?"

"Yes, of course. I will make the request right away. Just be ready."

Finally! We could possibly arrive in Colombia within another week or two! Sadly, all the adoption rules changed significantly since the last family's successful appeal. They appealed, won, and stayed to complete the adoption. We would have to travel once to appeal, return home to await approval, complete more paperwork and finally travel again, months later, to complete the actual adoption.

I informed my substitute of every little change, which I'm sure drove her crazy. As much as I wanted to appear as a responsible teacher, I couldn't keep it up. My teammates finally told me I couldn't keep trying to over plan. We all teach the same things, anyway, so they offered to pass on their own lesson plans to my substitute in my absence.

So many details to think about! We contacted David's teachers to explain the possibility of him traveling soon. We also made sure a room still remained available at the adoption hotel in Colombia. I even started to pack! We just needed an actual date to purchase the airline tickets.

Is this real? I trusted God moved things along quickly now. I didn't want to guard my heart. I only wanted to board a plane for Colombia as soon as possible.

In the meantime, Juan David struggled with intense anxiety, although he didn't know anything about the situation with our case. I tried to call him one evening, but he wasn't there. The male house parent took advantage of my call to talk with me pretty seriously about him for the first time.

"He's really anxious about you coming for him. He longs to be with your family." His voice spoke so kindly to me, but his words made me as anxious as Juan David, longing to get this process over with.

"We are doing everything we can to make the adoption possible, but the process is difficult and complicated. Can I call him later this evening?" Since I couldn't talk frankly with Juan David about the adoption, it felt good to explain our efforts to the man who lived with him.

"Of course. Your phone calls always lift his spirits." He knew how much we loved that boy. His final comment encouraged me.

I called later, but I only heard a busy signal. When I finally got through, Juan David had already fallen asleep.

I felt horrible. A female house parent answered this time, so I asked if I could possibly call during the weekend.

"Yes, that will be fine. You can call around eight o'clock tomorrow morning." Her kind voice set me at ease.

I called Juan David the next morning right at eight o'clock. We shared a sweet conversation, but he sounded sad. "Your house parent told me you're having a rough time. I'm sorry you feel so anxious. I promise you I will come." I didn't promise I'd adopt him, just that I'd come. In fact, I assumed at that moment we'd head to Colombia within the next two weeks.

Not my smartest move. Actually, one of the worst decisions I could have made in the whole process. Now I unintentionally played with his heart.

I explained again that I couldn't promise anything regarding an adoption. "You know we want to adopt you, but we don't make the final decision. Both of our governments need to agree on the best situation for you."

However, the boy still wanted me to know how he would help around the house, with all the chores, etc. He already claimed the adoption as reality.

Little did I know at the time that children from his orphanage traveled to the States every year, and almost all of them found families. No wonder he seemed to know more than what I even told him. He knew how it worked, but in his young world, it took way too long.

Unfortunately, we didn't get to go to Colombia a week later. The main psychologist who denied our case left for a vacation, so the committee recommended we not try to appeal without him there.

Sigh. Our agency's director asked when we could go, and they said they hoped to give us a date within a few days.

So much for using Mike's vacation time. Life remained in limbo, and I could hardly keep going with life so up in the air. Our faith stayed strong, but our flesh grew weaker with each passing moment.

Juan David seemed more settled after our last conversation. September just began, but Halloween already occupied his mind! We often compared our cultures and customs, so he wanted to tell me all about how they celebrate Halloween, his favorite holiday.

"I love to dress up in costumes. Can you send me one? Please?"

I never sent a package to Colombia because it could easily cost hundreds of dollars. If you attempt a more inexpensive option, your package could take months to arrive, if it arrived at all. However, I said I would look for costumes to send him before Halloween. I thought for sure I'd fly to Colombia before then at least to appeal, so I figured I'd take the costume with me.

That sweet boy also said his house parent agreed to let me keep calling the kids together on Saturday afternoons, so I did. I even put them on speaker phone so Mike and David could hear them. They seemed happiest whenever I called them together. I cherished Saturday afternoons, knowing I could talk to them and also hear their voices interacting with each other.

I didn't realize Julian stood in the background each time, watching them interact with me over the phone. He saw their faces light up when they heard my voice, and he witnessed how much they adored me. Sadly, I never took into account what all he might suffer, knowing he'd lose them soon. They would gain a new family while he lost the only family he had left.

Neither Juan David nor Viviana mentioned Julian very much. Viviana shares a birthday month with Julian, her birthday only four days after his. On her birthday earlier in the year, she'd said her brother Juan David had a present for her. When I asked Juan David about the present, he said his brother had the money to buy it, not him. The first I'd really heard about Julian, now I knew he had a job and a way to make money.

Now, almost six months later, Juan David suddenly talked more about Julian. "If you adopt me, can I call my brother and send him letters?"

We, of course, planned to let them have as much contact with their brother as we could afford financially. We knew we likely wouldn't be able to visit him often in Colombia because of the expense, but we wanted to encourage any other form of communication between them.

The silence regarding our appeal, though, wreaked havoc on me emotionally. I clung to scripture and to Christian song lyrics like never before. I journaled about everything God taught me. His fingerprints smothered this story. Yet the days just passed by, keeping my children separated from a mother who wanted to love all over them.

They soon granted me permission to talk to Juan David three different nights a week, plus Saturdays. I thanked God for the kindness his house parents showed me. I cherished each phone call with those kids, and now e-mails from Juan David, too. I knew God kept our channel of communication wide open for a reason.

In the meantime, I searched for Halloween costumes in several stores. I also kept an eye out for something small to add to the Halloween package that he could open on his birthday six days later. I never imagined we wouldn't arrive in Colombia by then, November 6, his twelfth birthday. He came to Texas at the age of ten!

Halloween costumes, unfortunately, come with a pretty high price tag attached! I knew sending the box alone might cost a small fortune, so I searched for a cheaper route with the actual costumes. David and I browsed the local thrift store and enjoyed picking out costumes. David picked one for himself, too, while he searched for one for Juan David. I eyed the shelves and aisles for a simple princess dress for Viviana.

I couldn't decide, so I bought two. David found matching costumes in different sizes for him and Juan David. I looked at him and smiled. "It's almost like you're brothers."

"Mommy, we are already brothers."

Wow. I loved observing the faith of a child with no doubt in his mind. On Halloween, night he and Juan David would wear matching outfits just like brothers, even in separate countries. I knew Juan David would like knowing that, too. He seemed to adore David, and they had so much in common.

During a recent conversation with Juan David, we talked about the distance between Dallas and Austin, where we lived in comparison to where he stayed for the hosting program. He didn't have a map of Texas to look at, so I explained that Austin lay situated a few hours south of Dallas. I searched all over for a small sentimental gift to send for his birthday, and I recalled our conversation about the cities when my eyes caught sight of a little blue keychain shaped like Texas. Tiny diamonds imbedded themselves in the location of all the major cities, including Dallas and Austin, like a little map. I knew it made the perfect gift, a tangible reminder of the two families in Texas that loved him.

I never expected the surprise God neatly tucked around the next corner. Mid-October already, we still didn't have a date to appeal. While I checked my e-mail on a break at work, I noticed a message from Julian! I quickly opened it and read the most priceless note I'd ever received.

"Hello, Rachelle. How are you? I hope you are well. I only want to thank you for making the decision to adopt my brother and sister. I want to ask you to please do everything possible so you can adopt them, and when they are with you, I ask you to please show them a lot of love, all the love they did not receive from our mother. I give you a thousand thanks and hope you are filled with blessings."

Imagine the courage it took him to write that. Already sixteen years old, he couldn't be included in the adoption (at least that's what they told us). He must have gotten my e-mail address from his brother, who only had it for a few short weeks. I considered this letter his blessing for us to become their new family, an earnest plea and attempt to help them. What an act of selfless love toward his siblings!

I wrote him back immediately, telling him the same thing I told Juan David—both governments needed to agree on the placement before they made a final decision. It was not our decision to make at this point. I assured him we continued to do everything in our power to see them again. His siblings already had my love, and I loved him, too. I appreciated his e-mail more than he would ever know. I vowed to keep him a constant, steady presence in their lives once we got them home.

"Okay, God, what role does this boy play in our story? Will you use him to help us bring them home? Does any chance exist to adopt him, too, to get all three of them together? I assume he connects more to this story than we know. You've held things off long enough for him to finally make contact with us. We obviously didn't see this coming . . ."

Part Two
TO THE VALLEY...

FALLING APART

"My guilt has overwhelmed me like a burden too heavy to bear."
Psalm 38:4

If Only I Could Tell You

Up early on this cold fall morn
just sitting here thinking of you,
knowing how much you long to come here,
and how much I long to go there, too.

I can't imagine what you go through
each and every day,
knowing a family has already chosen you,
yet not understanding the delay.

Your brother wrote me a heartfelt plea
to press on to bring you home.
He asked me to always love you
in a way you've never been shown.

Your sister touched a nerve
when she asked about her room,
not knowing it belonged to her,
nor that it's awaited her since June.

You sounded so down and quiet
as you wrote my name down on your page.
Did you crave that love of a mother
that you lost at a very young age?

When I learn contentment in the waiting,
the three of you tug on my heart strings.
If only I could tell you
all we have been doing.

If only you knew the whole story
of this journey to bring you home.
I cling to my dreams of that day,
hoping it will soon come.

October 17, 2009. Nearly fourteen months had passed since Juan David and Viviana returned to Colombia after spending a summer in Austin, Texas. They still lived in an orphanage in Bogotá, while our home right outside of Dallas, Texas awaited them. I left the local Mail Mart to send them their first package from us, containing a karate outfit Juan David requested, Halloween costumes for both kids, and something small for Julian. I also tucked in a small envelope with a birthday card for Juan David and the little keychain inside. I wrote on the envelope, "Do not open until your birthday!"

"I promise. I promise I won't open it early." He assured me I could trust him to wait until his birthday. He acted giddy just knowing a package headed his way.

I wanted more than anything to deliver it in person, but I knew I couldn't wait any longer to send it. It cost us a fortune, as I expected, but you can't put a price on knowing how happy and loved it made them feel.

I sent him an e-mail that evening to tell him I sent the package. He replied the next morning.

"Thank you! I miss you, and I hope to be with you soon. From: your adoptive son."

He also sent pictures, giving me my first chance to "see" him since he returned to Colombia in August of the previous year. He'd definitely grown and matured some. What a beautiful boy! Oh, how I hoped his closing words soon rang true, for him to officially become my adoptive son. I couldn't even fathom how his heart would shatter if it didn't come to pass.

I struggled to connect on the phone with both kids throughout the following week. Thankfully, Julian sent me an e-mail a few days later thanking me for the gifts, so I knew the package arrived safely.

My heart, however, grew more fragile every day. I drove to work in tears every single morning, my faith challenged almost beyond the limit through this inexplicable wait. I didn't understand why it took so long to give us a date to go down there. Yet we received no response from Colombia whatsoever.

Just silence. Absolute silence.

Yet in that silence, God let me grow even closer to these two, no, three children every week. I never expected to build a relationship with their older brother, too! His e-mails reminded me of God's constant presence and complete control. He still worked out his ultimate plan.

So why couldn't we go down there already?

Scared

Some days I feel like crying,
other days my heart just aches,
I miss them terribly,
terrified I'll have to let them go.

I don't know what to think,
I don't know how to feel,
I don't know what to believe,
or if I should even hold on.

I hurt so deep inside
as I continue to wait
for that final proclamation
of who my family is meant to be.

I thought I heard it clearly,
Confident we obeyed the call.
But now my heart is torn,
hoping we didn't misread it all.

What is really going on?
Had they even seen our letters yet?

How long before we hear
What step we need to take?

Will there even be a next step?
Or should I not hold on to false hope?
I'm crumbling inside, falling apart.
The truth is, I'm scared.

October 30. The day before Halloween and Mike's birthday, I received a message on my phone from our agency's director.

"Call me back as soon as you can."

I didn't get a single chance to call her until two o'clock in the afternoon on my conference time.

"Are you sitting down, Rachelle?"

Colombia responded finally. The committee over our case decided not to give us a date to appeal in person because they refused to reconsider our adoption petition. After fourteen months of living on the edge with our lives turned upside down, pouring every bit of our hearts and lives into two orphaned children, the door closed.

No reason.

No explanation.

Case closed.

Is it really over, just like that? Do we have any thread of hope left? My heart crashed to the floor, scattering emotions all over the place. Her words sucked everything out of me. I could barely breathe.

"We're not giving up yet. We'll send our representative back one more time to see if they will give you a chance to let one of their own psychologists do a new psychological evaluation." She hinted at a small ray of hope.

I felt completely defeated. I put my head down on my desk and let the tears fall. Devastated.

Hundreds of prayers went up on our behalf and on the kids' behalf for God to change the adoption committee's heart toward us. I even prayed for the two men in particular by name. For reasons I couldn't begin to understand, God didn't soften their hearts at all. They still believed us incapable of parenting an adopted child.

We failed those children.

Halloween didn't hold the fun we'd anticipated. Rather than celebrate Mike's birthday, we spent the weekend in shock with no hope of climbing out of our misery.

Only two days before, Juan David came to the phone giddy with excitement over receiving the package he'd requested for so long. A package that contained the costume connecting him to David that night and the gift for the birthday he longed to spend at home with us.

Now I could only wonder what the picture looked like on his side. Did anyone tell him? If not yet, who would break the news to him? What would they say? When?

What about Viviana? Could I still visit her like I promised? Could I send her the suitcase full of goodies she'd requested over the last six months?

What about Julian? I didn't even know where he fit into the picture, yet I felt so confident he played a key role in this adoption. Did I have any hope to hold on to? Would I ever talk to them again? A million questions and thoughts ran through my head, but those kids held my utmost concern, along with David's fragile heart.

Had we been fools all along, and sadly, at the expense of these children? How could I ever forgive myself for leading them on for so long?

Messing With Their Hearts

How do I pick up the pieces?
Where do I go from here?
Was this really your plan all along?
I thought it looked so clear.

So many pieces to this puzzle,
yet they all don't seem to fit.
Is there another puzzle out there
with a different picture set?

Did we do something wrong?
Is there more we still don't know?
Is this the final answer?
I don't know how to take this blow.

Do I keep looking for a miracle,
or do I allow my heart to grieve?
Have we exhausted every outlet,
or is there still hope left to retrieve?

What is going on here?
God, there are children's hearts at stake!
Did our love only give false hope
That now will have to break?

I had to keep holding on. As long as my agency didn't give up, I wouldn't either. I couldn't let go until every remaining chance disappeared. I fell to my knees and begged anyone and everyone to do the same, to pray for a miracle to bring my children home to me—where they belonged.

Perhaps we could see a Colombian psychologist. Maybe the committee could arrange a phone call with our own psychologist via translators. Maybe, just maybe, God would still intervene.

He got us this far, right? He wouldn't keep communication with the kids open this long, allowing us to grow closer every day, only to let it all fall apart. He wouldn't do that. Would he?

Until someone broke the news to the kids, I held firmly to that faith. My God was big enough to move this huge mountain standing in front of us.

Despite my faith, my whole world crashed down only a few days later when I received a third e-mail from Julian.

"Thank you so much for everything you did to try to adopt my siblings. Even though it didn't work out, my brother and sister will never forget you. We are all very sad after watching their dreams to join your family crumble. I hope God will fill your lives with many blessings. Juan David and Viviana will always love you."

No!!!! This can't be happening. Not yet! It's only been three days! My eyes filled with tears right there in the computer lab at school, still fairly early in the morning. I don't know how in the world I hid them from my students for the remainder of the day.

My agency said they wouldn't give up yet, but now that I knew someone told the kids, everything inside me hurt. A heaviness fell upon my spirit and refused to lift. I felt so helpless. We did everything in our power to keep them from ever hearing those heart-wrenching words, yet we couldn't stop it from happening.

We failed them. The guilt I carried with me from that day forward nearly sucked the breath out of me.

Mike still waited for a miracle. He's the optimist in our family. Our agency continued to fight for another chance, or at least that's what they said. I, personally, gave up the fight.

Racked with guilt, I imagined how the kids struggled on their side of the equation. Viviana lost the "tía" who planned to visit and bring her presents. She would be sad, but she would survive. Julian lost his dream of seeing his siblings adopted together so they could have a brighter future, but now they stayed with him for longer than he expected, so he would be okay, too.

But Juan David lost the family he already assumed himself a part of. He lost the one person he convinced himself was his mom, the man he claimed as a dad, and the little boy he already considered his younger brother. He couldn't wait for his adoption. He'd watched many of his friends in the orphanage come and go, either to reunite with their biological families or join a new family through adoption. His turn finally looked so close ... and now further away than ever. My heart ached for him. Helpless, I couldn't do a thing.

Without Julian, I never would have known anyone told the kids we weren't coming, after all. No one in Colombia ever told us, nor did they communicate any such information with our agency.

I didn't know what to do. I normally called both of the kids on Wednesday evenings. My stomach tied itself in knots all day, while I tried to decide whether or not to still call.

Did I just drop them?

I couldn't. What would that do to them?

I had to try.

I nervously dialed Juan David's number that evening. I sensed hesitation in the normally kind female voice that answered the phone, but she still passed the phone to him.

The sadness in his voice broke my heart. I'd gotten so accustomed to him coming to the phone singing or cracking jokes. Not this time. He didn't say much. I did a lot of prompting, but until somebody from Colombia (besides Julian) told me what the kids knew, I acted like I didn't know anything changed.

"You sound sad. Is something wrong?" I desperately hoped he'd tell me what he knew, but he didn't.

"It's just something my brother said to me yesterday that bothered me." I knew exactly what his brother told him, but I couldn't say anything. I didn't keep him on the phone long, just long enough to tell him I loved him. Except this time, he didn't respond.

That phone call tore me apart.

I said I'd call him again two days later on his birthday. He promised me he didn't open his gift yet. I called Viviana that evening, as well, but she seemed oblivious. It was different with her.

Two days later, Juan David turned twelve. I woke up early

that morning with him heavy on my heart. I imagined him opening that little gift he'd been so excited about only a week earlier. A gift I carefully picked to fill him with hope about his future life and family in Texas. Now, it served as the opposite, a reminder of a shattered dream. He hoped for an adoption before his birthday. I never imagined it could take that long or that it might never happen at all.

I still called both kids that evening. Viviana continued to show her giddy, curious little self over the phone. Her house parent didn't even hesitate to pass the phone to her to let her talk to me.

When I tried to call Juan David, the lady at his house said he went to the dentist. I called back later in the evening, and I did get to talk to him on his birthday. (I called the night before, but they said someone took him to get his hair cut.) The lady who answered the phone seemed different when I asked for him this time, a bit hesitant to pass the phone to him, but she did. It made me wonder how many more times she would let me call.

Thankfully, Juan David did not seem as heavy-hearted as two days prior. His normal, talkative self reappeared on the other end of the line.

"Happy birthday!"

"Thank you." I could sense a smile on his end of the line.

"Did you open your present this morning?"

"Yes, thank you for the keychain. I clipped it onto my pants all day today." He told me his brother planned to give him a gift the following day. That led into a conversation about opportunities the orphanage gives to the older kids so they can earn money to spend on personal things.

We only talked for about fifteen minutes. Mike and David got on the phone to tell him happy birthday, too.

"Good-bye, Sweetie. I love you, and I miss you."

"Good-bye. I miss you and love you, too." Little did I know it was our last time to say good-bye. I continued to call every week, but they never passed him the phone again.

All the hoping, dreaming, and believing things would be final by his birthday, final they were. Yet not the finality we hoped for.

I continued to call Viviana, and they always let her talk to me. Her house coordinators treated me with such kindness. She lived in a loud environment, so I did a lot of listening. I no longer understood my purpose in her life, but I loved her still the same. God built that relationship for a reason.

"Tía, is your son there? Please tell him I love him." She felt connected to all of us.

The next time I called, she said, "Tell your husband I miss him." I wanted nothing more than to give that little girl the biggest hug ever.

"Okay, Sweetheart. I will tell him. Please tell your brothers I love them." I couldn't stop thinking about Julian's sudden involvement in the story. I didn't know him that well yet, but I loved him, too.

When I called Juan David's home, I got a different answer every time. On Wednesday night, they said, "Oh, I'm sorry. He's at the doctor this evening." On Friday, "He stayed at school to celebrate an end of year school function."

"Oh. Can I call him later?" I asked.

"I don't think so tonight. I really don't know when he will get home." I'd called many times throughout the year on evenings he wasn't there, but it rarely happened twice in one week. I suspected they didn't want me to talk to him anymore, but the kindness in the lady's voice always threw me off. I didn't know what to think.

Mike kept his hope alive, believing God still held a miracle. Our agency seemed to do more to fight for us than ever before. Looking back now, I should have demanded direct contact with the agency's lawyer. So many aspects of our case could have and should have been handled differently. But out of pure naivety, we didn't know any better.

I already gave up the fight in my heart. Deep down, I couldn't keep holding on. I had to let myself grieve, and I needed to help my son grieve this loss, as well.

David couldn't even begin to understand what happened.

"Mommy, it all made sense. Juan David loves what I love. I love what he loves. . . . Their decision doesn't connect."

He suddenly felt lonely. Thinking about the fact that Juan David and Viviana weren't coming home, after all, made him aware for the first time of how much he looked forward to their coming. My heart broke for him.

I had to release myself from the process to offer my full presence to David. He needed me to hang out with him, play games with him, and enjoy our days together, the way we always spent our summers, just the two of us. Only now, we both carried a huge void inside us everywhere we went.

Somehow we all put on a brave smile to enthusiastically celebrate David's birthday the next week. We spent more money than normal this time, knowing he needed the extra attention and focus. We told him we couldn't afford things due to the adoption expenses far too many times. We didn't dare use that excuse for his birthday now. We bought him the Wii he'd wanted for so long, went out for pizza, and celebrated with our close friends. God blessed us with good memories of his birthday, preparing us for the hard days that quickly followed.

Four days later, on November 20, we reached the end of the road regarding the adoption. The committee in Colombia told the agency's representative we couldn't do anything more. Their final decision held firm. Despite all of our prayers, Juan David and Viviana would not be coming home.

I had no words. I couldn't make sense of anything we went through over the last year and a half or why God even let our paths cross with those two precious children. I went numb. The hurt cut deeper than anything I'd ever experienced in my life. I felt like the biggest failure. My heart couldn't handle all the emotions it held. Embarrassment. Humiliation. Devastation. Guilt. Depression. Overwhelming grief. Confusion.

I felt so lost.

My phone rang while we ate dinner out that evening, but I

didn't answer it. I put my phone up to my ear to listen to the message my mom left on my voicemail.

"Honey, I just wanted to say how so very sorry I am." She cried through the message, as did I. Tears streamed down my cheeks the entire evening. So numb, I couldn't talk to anyone. I never even called back. I may have already given up fighting nearly three weeks before, but hearing the absolute finality of our case still tore me apart. Not a shred of hope remained.

What in the world was it all for?

GRIEVING

"O God, you are my God, earnestly I seek you; my soul thirsts for you, my body longs for you, in a dry and weary land where there is no water." Psalm 63:1

My Sincerest Apologies

My heart is once again in pieces,
and there's no sense to all this mess.
How could loving two abandoned children
turn into such a hopeless quest?

We gave it all we had to give,
faithful to the call.
We made every preparation,
yet ran straight into a wall.

This time they say it's final,
the decision has been made.
Much to all of our surprise,
Their first decision stayed.

My little ones, can I tell you
How deeply sorry I am?
How I wish to turn the hands of time
back to where this all began.

All the hope we intended to give you
actually took your hope away.
Now I can hardly believe
you aren't coming home someday.

If we had never met you,
you'd surely have a family by now.
I'm sorry we held you back,
that your home has not been found.

Deep down in my heart,
I know God still has a plan.
But why you had to lose a family twice,
I don't think I'll ever understand.

Only a few days remained before Thanksgiving. My parents visited us every year for the holiday, but I didn't look forward to being around anyone. How could I celebrate this holiday season? I was a mess. I struggled to know my purpose, my place, my identity.

When you believe something for so long, your whole reality revolves around that belief. I believed those two children from Colombia were my children. That belief consumed me, along with everything involved to turn it into reality. Now, suddenly I had to backtrack and try to remember life without them, before them.

My faith a shattered mess, I tried to convince myself God purposed this all for a reason he had not yet revealed. I tried to keep my head up. We stayed busy and distracted so we wouldn't have to face the ugly reality that we failed.

I didn't know how to grieve. I didn't know what it felt like, what we should do, or how we were supposed to act. I went through the motions of everyday life. I went to work each day, put on a brave (fake) smile, did my job and stayed as busy as I possibly could. I avoided eye contact with anyone because I couldn't let people see the tears welled up in my eyes all day long, every day.

Our Eyes Can't Lie

It couldn't be more obvious
by the twinkle in my eye,
how dearly I loved them.
No, our eyes just cannot lie.

People said my eyes sparkled
whenever I spoke of them.
They'd become so precious to me,
as priceless as a gem.

I saw them as a gift,
given directly from God to me.
I cherished every moment
leading toward our forever family.

The day I heard the news,
I tried so hard to hide the pain.
I didn't want to face anyone
or answer questions I couldn't explain.

Yet one voice gently told me,
she'd seen through my disguise.

She suspected we didn't have good news
because of the sadness in my eyes.

Now I find myself avoiding
looking anyone in the eye.
I still don't have any answers
or explanations to the why's.

I'm trying hard to keep walking,
(though I feel like running away),
but the hurt cuts so deep,
the directions seem so gray.

I don't know where I'm going,
Nor where I am to turn.
I don't know what to make of this,
nor what I am supposed to learn.

If by chance you're a lucky one
To get a glimpse into my eye,
you'll have no need to ask
because my eyes just cannot lie.

The tears streamed down my face as soon as I slipped into my car after a long day at work. I cried the whole way home nearly every single day. Nothing in the world made sense to me.

I probably should have talked to someone, but I didn't know what to say. I didn't know how to articulate the conflicting feelings raging inside. In fact, I didn't even know what really went on inside me.

I should have taken advantage of my mom visiting, ready and willing to give me a shoulder to cry on, but I didn't. I should have joined a grief support group, but a failed adoption lies in a category of its own. You're grieving a death, even though no one ever died. I should have talked with a counselor, but I didn't. I should have opened up to someone, but I didn't.

I did build a huge wall around myself. I pushed everyone away, and I didn't let anyone in.

My husband and I should have talked and comforted one another more, but we didn't. We each grieved in our own way. I expressed my pain and confusion in the only way I knew how, with pen and paper. I drafted poems on any scrap of paper I found lying around. I scribbled prayers. I wrote letters to God in my journals.

Writing brought me comfort and kept me sane, so I wrote as often as possible.

How Did We Get Here?

So much on my heart,
thoughts racing through my mind,
so many questions without answers
as I turn and look behind.

I'd never been so sure of anything
than the fact that they were mine.
So fully convinced
God chose me as their mom.

They were meant to be the siblings
of my one and only son.
God meant for me to raise them,
to pick up where their mother left off.

They made a perfect match for us,
we made the perfect match for them.
Our puzzle pieces fit right together.
The picture looked so clear.

We earned favor in all the right eyes,
so how did that get us here?

With nowhere to run and no place to hide, I could not escape the pain of our new reality. I saw reminders of those kids everywhere I went. Just walking down the toy aisle at my favorite store felt like someone stabbed a knife through my heart. The sight of all those sweet, little girl toys and princess clothes killed me inside because I knew I no longer had a chance to buy them for my own little girl.

Passing any random garage sale felt like a slap in the face, reminding me how much time and effort we invested into three yard sales to raise money for the adoption. Dolls, clothes, and all of Viviana's color preferences occupied our spare bedroom at home. David's bunk beds held Juan David's special blanket, while the empty bunk screamed of his absence. Clothing filled the closets in both rooms, clothes we'd either purchased or that someone donated for the kids. Their pictures covered wall after wall in our house, pictures I couldn't ever imagine taking down. They felt so permanent the day I placed them on the walls.

I hurt deeply for David. We put life on hold for the last year and a half. No vacations. No extra spending money. Nearly every penny went towards adoption expenses in some way. He didn't deserve to live like this. He sacrificed so much of himself, his family, and his life.

Now that the kids didn't come home, enough was enough. He wanted to forget about everything and move on. He hated watching me cry every single day with no end in sight. He detested the sadness we now carried with us as a family. He couldn't stand the emptiness inside.

He struggled with intense anger. He resented Colombia for not letting us appeal in person and for misinterpreting our parenting abilities by saying we didn't have a strong bond with him. He wanted to tell them how wrong they were about his mommy and daddy. He harbored anger toward our agency for not advocating for us enough or communicating with us like they should have. He dealt with more anger yet toward the summer hosting program for bringing the kids to the States, allowing them to cross our path and change our lives forever.

He dealt with even more anger toward God. His now eight-year-old mind couldn't process this turn of events. How could God let us proceed, so convinced of something that would never happen? David's faith stood so strong through it all, and now it fell into a million pieces.

Mike stayed pretty quiet, actually keeping us from completely falling apart. He kept David and me from going over the edge or completely exploding from everything built up inside. His hurt showed differently. His eyes and voice expressed a sadness that hadn't been there before.

We lost that joy of knowing our purpose. We all wanted someone to blame, but, as much as we hated to admit it, we could only point our fingers up toward Heaven. It didn't matter who made the mistakes. God's arm could have reached down and placed those children with us. His sovereignty could have changed everything.

If he meant for them to be with us, they would be here. A faulty agency, a poorly translated word, or a misinterpreted personality assessment couldn't trump God's will. He let this happen. We each wrestled on our own with God and our faith.

If I looked back now and admitted we read the signs all wrong and followed a road never meant for us to travel, then I'd have to accept as pure coincidence every little "glimpse" of God we saw along the way. How could we explain the miracles we'd witnessed with our finances or all the furniture and travel provisions? What about the heart changes, unexpected opportunities, necessary relationships, and timely friendships?

If I didn't hear God's voice clearly, then how would I ever know how to listen for his voice again? Our clear picture now seemed like a puzzle with pieces scattered all over the place. The pieces didn't match or fit together anymore. Some looked destroyed or disfigured, and others went completely missing, leaving the puzzle impossible to complete.

Either I accepted God never led us down this path and therefore disregard my entire faith along the way, or I accepted that God did lead us down this very road, straight into the heartache we now lived. Neither one made a pretty picture. Neither one made sense.

Up until this point in my life, my relationship with God grew more intimate every day. I cherished my morning time of prayer more than any other time of the day. I longed to spend time with my Creator, pouring my heart out to him while interceding often for others. As I grew closer to Christ every year, I found nothing else could even compare. I felt like a miserable, unsatisfied mess when I missed that hour in the mornings. My Savior's love filled me and refreshed me every morning.

Now, for the first time in my entire life, I felt so unloved. I didn't understand why my faith wasn't enough. My mornings no longer felt "romantic and peaceful." The intimate conversation stopped.

Daily screaming matches in my car became my only conversations with God. Me screaming about my anger, humiliation, hurt, confusion, and devastation. I felt offended and insulted. He, on the other hand, took it all, carried me through it and gave me enough strength to keep moving each day. He gently whispered in my ear that, yes, despite it all, I could still trust him.

He did love me, and he actually hurt, too, knowing the extent of the pain in my heart. It hurt him to see me hurting. He missed me, and even if I wouldn't admit to it, I really missed him, too.

Truly, my anger mostly directed itself inward. We all fought through anger toward ourselves for not being "good enough" for the committee to approve us in the first place, forcing us to let the kids down. The guilt overwhelmed us at times, like a heavy weight crushing us beneath it. So great a heaviness, I could barely even breathe.

I let them down. I didn't fight hard enough or stand firm enough. I must not have spoken or written to express our case clearly. I didn't do everything I could have done.

What doors had we not opened or gone through that could have made a difference? Did we open and go through doors we shouldn't have? Those precious siblings counted on us, and we let them down. Where exactly did it all go wrong? Did one specific thing trigger their whole chain reaction against us? Could we have done something differently to avoid this whole mess? Did we ever even stand a chance or did doom follow our case from the beginning?

Not only did we fail the kids, we failed everyone involved. We could compile a running list of everyone we let down:

- The summer hosting program
- Our adoption agency
- The kids' host family
- The families not chosen to pursue this adoption
- Everyone who donated money
- The organizations that awarded us grant money
- Our church's Adoption Ministry

Basically we failed everyone who supported our entire journey.

In addition to bearing the weight of failing so many, we also knew we failed each other, and we failed our son.

Grief traveled more levels than I knew. We mourned the loss of the kids' presence in our lives, along with the loss of an assumed reality. We also grieved for them, knowing only a fraction of their loss. They lost a set of parents, a new brother, grandparents, aunts, uncles, and cousins. They ultimately lost the security of a forever family, now for the second time.

We grieved the loss of a dream, as well as our ability to fulfill a promise to the kids and to our son. We grieved losing our joy and purpose, along with our confidence and faith. We even grieved the loss of finances we gave up so willingly for what seemed to now be "nothing."

Grief took over our lives for several months. I thank God for numbing us to different levels of pain so we didn't have to experience them all at once. He let us grieve one stage at a time, strengthening us to endure the next one. Still faithful, God carried us through it all. He never left us alone or abandoned us.

After continuing to call Juan David once a week for a solid month only to hear excuses each time as to why he wasn't there, I finally got the point. They no longer allowed him to talk with me, so I stopped calling. I could only hope he knew I tried. I always wondered who finally told him why the phone calls stopped. How did he react? Who comforted him in his grief? What exactly did they tell him? Maybe Julian could share those things with me someday if we stayed in contact, or maybe I'd never know the answers to those questions on this side of Heaven.

To my surprise, my contact stayed alive and intact with Viviana throughout my grieving period as I continued to call her faithfully every week.

"Tía, will you please come to see me for Christmas?"

"I don't know if I can get permission to see you at Christmas, but I will send you a special package if I don't make it to visit you." I felt awkward still calling her, especially since I no longer understood God's purpose for these conversations. He obviously still wanted me in her life for some reason.

My phone calls must have meant the world to her. I adored her and loved hearing the sound of her sweet voice. Until she had a mother of her own, I counted her as a daughter in my heart.

One evening in early December, she asked me to pass the phone to David and Mike. Mike took the phone and heard her say, "Te quiero (I love you)."

He naturally responded in his limited Spanish, saying he loved her, too. Then he quickly handed the phone back to me.

"He said he loves me!!!!" She nearly cried into the phone, repeating herself several times.

Priceless. Hearing Mike say he loved her touched her deeply. She never had a father in her life to show her such affection.

I will never forget that conversation with her. Sadly, I never heard her sweet voice again. A week later when I called, a female voice told me Viviana no longer had permission to receive phone calls. Words can't even begin to describe how much I would miss talking with that little girl.

I never dreaded Christmas as much as I did that year. The sadness in my heart stole any joy in celebrating the season. I purchased two beautiful blue Christmas stockings in the summertime to fill for my "newest" family members. Now they remained empty. I had no desire to dig out the other decorations, to transform our little house with the magic of Christmas. I didn't want a tree, a wreath, a star, lights … nothing. I hung our stockings and set out a few nativity scenes. My heart couldn't handle much more than that.

David, on the other hand, wanted and needed every decoration up. We dug out at least a few bins for him to go through, and he decorated his entire bedroom with several little trees, nativity sets, reindeer, lights, and musical decorations. He filled his room to the brim with the Christmas magic the rest of our home lacked.

Viviana clung to her dream of our visit, but we didn't have the opportunity to travel to Colombia see her. I kept my promise to her by sending a Christmas package, filled with as many of the clothes and little goodies we bought for her that fit into the box--a special purple quilt, red sunglasses, a purple watch, Scooby-Doo movies, and a few other things she asked for.

We also filled the box as tightly as possible with the clothing we picked out for her at various yard sales throughout the year. I filled all the extra space with small dolls and toys, squeezed in a little white stuffed puppy, and even added a few Spanish books. On top of the box's contents, I placed a letter reminding her I would love her forever and would pray for her every day. A Christmas ornament with my picture on one side and David's picture on the other tucked itself inside the letter. The overflowing box represented my final good-bye.

Another box filled with clothes, books, and two backpacks also made its way toward Colombia for Juan David and Julian. I didn't know Juan David's size, so I suggested he and Julian split the contents based on what they needed, wanted, and could wear.

It both broke and thrilled my heart to include the special blanket he'd asked for, the one we draped over "his" bed. My final letter to him stated my sorrow over not spending Christmas with him, reminding him God still had a great plan. I never wrote the word "good-bye," but I knew he could read between the lines to know why I sent the box.

Mailing those two packages cost us a near fortune. One of us could have flown all the way to Colombia with them for a similar cost! But the money didn't matter. We knew those packages would light up their world for Christmas, as well as bring comfort to Juan David especially. Nothing mattered to me more.

School let out for the holiday; we mailed the boxes to Colombia, and then we headed out of town the same day. I don't know that any of us could have handled the holiday at home, even David, despite his room bursting at the seams with Christmas décor. Too many reminders of our shattered dreams would have made for a miserable vacation. David needed us fully present with him, and we needed to find a way to somehow enjoy ourselves.

After driving more than twelve hours straight through the night to Indiana, it felt good to distract ourselves with an early Christmas celebration with Mike's family for a few days. God even sent a special treat for David as soon as we arrived. Snow! Only an inch or two of accumulation was enough for David to blissfully throw snowballs and make snow angels.

A few days later, we continued our drive eastward all the way to Pennsylvania. A winter snowstorm hit right before we got there, so you can imagine the surprise that greeted David as we pulled up to nineteen inches of snow at my brother's house! Our little Texan never saw or played in so much snow in his entire life!

What an amazing ten days lay in front of our little boy. We showed him some of his mommy's old stomping grounds in Lancaster County. We also spent a day in Philadelphia, saw the Liberty Bell, and visited Hershey's Chocolate World. Yet the experiences in the snow, sledding, and building a huge snowman truly topped them all for David.

The time away did wonders for us, almost a therapeutic experience, constantly distracting us from our reality. Years had passed since I'd spent Christmas with my eldest brother, so I enjoyed the time to bond again with him and his family. I cherish the memories we made together.

Right before the New Year, we packed up again to head toward our last destination. We reserved a hotel room right outside of New York City, giving us the chance to spend New Year's Eve and New Year's Day exploring the Big Apple. The 9/11 Memorial site, as well as the beginning stages of the new Memorial Park, left David in awe and also filled him with great sadness. He still grew in my womb when the twin towers crumbled, so I didn't realize we'd never taken the time to tell him about that tragic day in America.

We felt lured into the festivities surrounding the infamous "ball drop" at midnight, though the weather and some unforeseen circumstances led us straight back to the comfort of our hotel and a television that evening.

We did nothing but explore more of the city on New Year's Day covering as much as we could on foot in a day. A long line already formed for the ferry ride to Ellis Island, so we decided to snap pictures of the Statue of Liberty from a distance rather than spend our time waiting in line. Instead, we hung out in Central Park for a few hours, taking in all the sights, and then inside the Museum of Natural History. The adventure of the city led us from place to place, hour by hour.

By the second day in January, we packed our things one final time to head back home to Texas. Mike drove twenty-two hours straight through, the entire way from New York City to Dallas. With only a day left to catch our breath and reorient ourselves, school and work called us back to reality quickly. Such a needed vacation, and I can't say I even wanted any extra time to rest or recuperate. It felt good to enjoy our family of three again, to build positive memories together after facing such negative ones recently.

Coming home at the beginning of a new year meant closing this last chapter of life to start a new one. The word "hard" can only begin to describe that process. Part of me still so bewildered by the chain of events over the last two years, I wanted to put the entire experience in a box, put the box on the shelf, and pretend it never existed or never happened, despite the reminders scattered everywhere. I didn't know how to interpret the contents of the box. If I put them away, maybe they'd make sense at a later time when I could emotionally handle bringing the box back down.

That, however, left me with a new problem. How did I go back to living life the way we did before them?

Those two kids changed me. They changed us. Our family before them no longer existed. We used to be whole, and now, we were broken. Once content with an only child, now something felt missing. We couldn't just go back in time.

They say it's better to have loved and lost than to have never loved at all. Part of me wished I'd never met them, both for our sakes and theirs. But the other part of me knew how amazing it felt to love them and be loved by them. Deep down, I knew I wouldn't trade that for anything in the world. But now what did I do with the huge void they left in my heart?

For a while, it helped to stay busy. We kept the calendar full of activities to keep some excitement alive in our life. Mike and I have always loved being involved in missions, as a pre-engaged, engaged, and married couple, so we eagerly signed up as a family to serve on the next church mission trip in California. We used the money we'd poured into savings for our adoption travels as a way to self-fund our endeavor.

Less than four weeks after coming home from the East coast, we found ourselves flying out to San Francisco on the West coast. Not only did we help a new church expand its ministry, but we made new friends from our own church and tasted a little bit of California culture. Exactly what we needed.

With our travels wrapped up and no new trips on the horizon, we knew we could use a big change at home. David lacked a companion now more than ever since his "siblings" didn't come home. Being an only child never bothered him before, but this new reality offered a screaming reminder that we had no sibling to offer our son. So, the search for a dog began.

An ad for a black lab caught our eye, reminding us of our two black labs in Indiana years earlier. David loved thinking about names for our new puppy.

"Maybe we could name him Rocky." David imagined his pup growing into a big, tough dog.

"Rocky sounds like a good name, but what about Mickey, since he's black?" I went for the fun names.

David and I went back and forth between the two names, finally deciding on Mickey. We drove out to pick Mickey up, and somehow I caved again. We came home not only with little Mickey, but with little Minnie, as well, the runt of the pack.

Those little pups added a lot of work and needed constant attention. Yet they filled part of the huge holes in our hearts and lives. We needed two of them, one of each gender, to help fill those voids the kids left behind. Now we had both a little girl dog and a little boy dog to take care of, nurture, and love—our valentines, home right in time for Valentine's Day.

So, what came next? A constant need existed to occupy our minds. This busyness and sense of adventure really did help dull the pain we felt deep within, or at least it helped us avoid dealing with it until a later time when we might handle it better emotionally. First we took a long vacation, far away from home, and then we headed out on a short mission trip, the very thing that made our hearts beat. After that, two precious little puppies filled our home with life again.

Suddenly the calendar didn't hold a single new activity or adventure. I didn't know how to handle that. Life started to dry up all over again.

My emotions didn't expect a rollercoaster ride through those dry months. Oh, how it hurt to attend a "baby shower" for a fellow teacher adopting two children. I still remembered when she expressed a tug on her heart to look into adoption after I announced our original plans to adopt from El Salvador. Now, over two years later, she adopted not one, but two children. We inspired her to start the process. Now, a son and daughter filled her arms, while mine felt emptier than ever.

One of the couples we met in Austin finally traveled to Colombia to complete their adoption of a child they met the same summer we met Juan David and Viviana. I felt thrilled for them, but reading their blog tore me up inside. They posted pictures of places we planned to visit. They stayed in the very place we arranged to stay. Those were supposed to be our pictures, our adventures, and our memories. Yet they reminded us now of pictures we'd never get to take, adventures we'd never experience, dreams that would not become realities, memories we'd never build.

I tried to settle back into life and work, but the emptiness quickly resurfaced. While I paid no attention, the music in me died. I found myself in a spiritual and emotional drought. In times past, I always had my poetry as an outlet, as sad as it might have been at times, to get me past each hump in the road, to help me connect my inner and outer worlds, to help me process and make sense of what life handed me.

Now I had nothing left in me to even try to write. Empty pages stared blankly at me. With no new goals to reach for and no new adventures in sight, this unforgettable loss hung over like a dark cloud. I began to die inside, another stage of the grief I didn't know would come.

EMPTINESS

"The Lord is close to the brokenhearted and saves those who are crushed in spirit." Psalm 34:18

I slowly realized the music inside me had indeed died. I tried so hard for so long to keep my head held high and to keep moving. My strength weakened daily and eventually disappeared. No passion or drive existed inside me. I lost all sense of purpose or mission. Without striving toward any new goals or dreams, the life inside me completely dried up, leaving me incredibly empty.

I had no words left to express, no song left in me to sing. I could write pages and pages, pouring out the contents of my heart, but the rhyme and the meaning didn't accompany them. My poems expressed the songs of my heart, yet I no longer had a reason to sing. Even when I sat down to write a poem, no words came. I sat in utter silence, staring at nothing but a blank page.

I felt even emptier inside when I couldn't write a single poem. But God used that barren feeling to let others' music speak to me on a deeper level than ever before in my life. I clung to music in a new way. Songs like Nicol Sponberg's "Resurrection"[1] truly expressed the cry of my heart for God to somehow create beauty out of the now shattered pieces of my heart. I desperately hoped God might breathe life back into me someday.

Christian contemporary music touched me deeply as I found myself relating so well to numerous songs. Many songs spoke directly to me, precisely describing my thoughts and feelings. If someone I never knew could write a song to articulate the depth of my heart so perfectly, I didn't walk this road alone. They walked a similar road, too. Maybe they hadn't faced the same circumstance, but they felt the same despair, connecting us. Their lyrics took a desperate heart and pointed it toward faith, giving me the hope I always found while writing my own poetry.

When I had no song left to write, God used others to write their music on my heart. What an impact these songwriters had on me to help me climb out of this lonely pit of grief.

At the same time, I also began to devour books. Pursuing Viviana and Juan David's adoption filled me with incredible joy and passion. I missed that joy. I craved it. I begged God every day to give it back to me. I read every book on joy I could get my hands on. In the mornings, I dug into Bible studies, learning scripture after scripture on the topic. I couldn't read enough books about grief and healing, hoping to gain some kind of headway on the stages that came with grief.

Little by little, God repaired my heart. He had to break me completely in order to mold me into the person he created me to be. My screaming matches subsided, and our relationship grew civil again. The intimacy didn't even come close to what it had once been, but deep down, I knew I could still trust him.

I knew and believed our experience had purpose. It could not have been for nothing. God didn't write the last page of our story yet. Meeting those children began something grander than

I could imagine, something that could never come to life had we not crossed paths with them. I clung to that. I had to.

Julian wrote me another sweet e-mail in March, three months since I had contact with any of them.

"My brother and sister miss you. They think of you a lot." Knowing they were okay helped me through this emotional drought, and I often wondered what I would have done if God didn't connect us with that precious brother right before it all fell through. Without him, I would have never known anything more about them.

Several months eventually passed by without any more word from Julian. Viviana's eighth birthday came in April of 2010, which meant Julian's seventeenth birthday also passed four days earlier. I couldn't send a gift or even a card since the orphanage officially cut off all my ties to them. They wanted the kids to let go of us in order to properly attach to the next family found for them. So, I sent my little princess a bouquet of prayers and kisses, and I asked others to send up a prayer for her, as well, to add to the beautiful bouquet.

I remembered thinking only a year earlier that she'd never spend another birthday without a mother because we'd complete her adoption before then. Unfortunately, she did celebrate her special day again without even the prospect of a mother in her life. As far as I knew, they hadn't matched another family to the kids yet.

When May approached and Julian didn't send another e-mail, I accepted in my heart that our communication ceased. God gave him to us to keep us informed enough about the kids to make it through those rough months. Now I needed to allow God to heal me so we could move on. As long as I knew more about them, I couldn't find closure to my grief. I thanked God a million times for that boy. Sending me a few simple e-mails did more for me than he ever knew. Yet now I let him go, too.

After sending a total of ten messages over a five-month period, Julian stopped writing to me. All three siblings now officially disappeared from our lives. I still dared to wonder if God might allow me to see them again someday. Would our paths ever cross again? Would we ever see our purpose for the role we'd played in their lives? Could a chance actually exist to someday meet Julian in person to thank him for what he did for us?

I counted it a blessing when I heard music beat in my heart again by the end of April that year. The passion and rhyme returned as poetry stirred within my soul. Words flowed from my pen, and I started to process and connect the recent past with the present and the future.

Still Walking . . .

Hearing your call
so loud and so clear,
we had no other choice
but to swallow our fear.

We took every step
as a step in the dark,
not knowing what followed,
or if we hit the mark.

Would we have enough money?
That was our number one doubt.
Yet we knew that our God
Already planned it all out.

Would we have enough patience
to handle the change?
Was this parenting challenge
completely out of our range?

Every question that surfaced
he answered with peace.
he placed a call on our lives,
thus our fears had to cease.

He provided the money,
we were never in need.
he provided other families
whose advice we could heed.

It all came together,
our lives were prepared.
We eagerly awaited
a challenge many wouldn't dare.

Yet all we prepared for,
all the needs God met,
all for a journey with
a destination we know not yet.

So we continue walking
one blind step at a time,
not knowing where we're headed,
or how steep remains the climb.

Even tragedy has a purpose,
so I continue to believe
God is still at work
while he gives me time to grieve.

Over time the anger within me subsided. I learned to accept the final outcome, even though my questions still begged for answers. My heart leaned more toward absolute surrender, and healing loomed closer than I knew.

The first weekend in May, I attended a spiritual retreat for women after a friend suggested it. I struggled with mixed feelings about the retreat. My husband attended the one for men the weekend before and came home different, almost like a new person. I knew I needed the time away, but I didn't know a soul there. Since

I'd already taken the time off of work and arranged for a substitute to cover my class for two days, I went, but reluctantly.

This retreat differed from any other retreat I attended in my life. The women did almost everything corporately, and the leaders packed the schedule tightly, leaving little room for reflection or time alone with God. However, God used a few periods of silence to speak to my heart.

I almost laughed when I heard the whole weekend themed around the concept of restoration.

"Okay, God, I'm listening. I've been on a quest for healing for the last seven months. I guess I'm exactly where you want me this weekend."

Once again, the songs hit a chord deep within my soul as we sang about God turning our weeping into dancing, lifting a weight of sadness from us to give us joy again. Would God do that for me? Did I still have a reason to sing?

I met some incredible ladies that weekend, and I found a kindred spirit who remains a dear friend even today. She and I connected almost immediately, and we barely spent a moment apart whenever we found a chance to hang out together. I thanked God for giving me this new, dear friend to help me continue through this journey.

Many tears spilled that weekend, which happens often on spiritual retreats, but not a single tear belonged to me. I watched others bear their hearts to one another and let go of hurts they held onto for far too long. Seeing their walls come down helped me realize how many walls I'd built up around myself. I suddenly saw how many people reached out to me over the last several months only to have me push them away.

My heart finally softened. I really didn't have to do this alone.

The final day of the retreat, God pressed heavily on my heart and asked me to trust him. I wanted so badly to grow in my faith again, but as long as I held on to my whys, my faith couldn't grow. I couldn't grow. I needed to trust him even if I never found answers.

Did I trust his character more than I trusted in his power to bring it all together?

Holding on to Juan David and Viviana kept me stuck in a miserable pit of self-pity. I knew they held me back from the growth I desperately wanted. I silently cried out to God that morning, finally surrendering those children to their Father who gave them to me in the first place.

"God, I do still trust you with them, even if I never know anything else about them. I trust you to give them the family they deserve." I felt like a huge weight lifted from my shoulders.

Our final hour, each woman shared how God spoke to her during the retreat. I stood there in front of everyone with tears finally streaming down my cheeks.

"I came here grieving the loss of two children after a failed adoption. These have been the hardest six months of my entire life. God took my faith at its strongest point and crushed it."

Then, without knowing where the words even came from, I continued, "But I believe he broke us, broke our family, in order to make something beautiful out of our story."

I did not realize God began to lift us out of the valley that very moment, carrying us right back up toward the mountain we confidently stood on a year ago.

Part Three
...AND BACK!

LATCHING ONTO HOPE

"I waited patiently for the Lord; he turned to me and heard my cry. He lifted me out of the slimy pit, out of the mud and mire; he set my feet on a rock and gave me a firm place to stand. He put a new song in my mouth, a hymn of praise to our God. Many will see and fear and put their trust in the Lord."
Psalm 40:1-3

Take Us to Colombia

After all of the heartache
and so many tears,
your purpose is finally
becoming a little more clear.

Could it be Colombia?
Is that where lies our ministry?
you asked me to love two of her children,
and now you gave me three.

I finally can see
maybe this all led to him,
but where we go from here . . .
I'm completely on a limb.

Less than ten months from now
He'll live completely on his own.
Please take us to Colombia
before he takes that step alone.

From everything he's told me
It's so clear he's in your hand,
We are the answer to his prayer
when he asked for strength to stand.

Please take us to Colombia
if that's where we're meant to be.
Please reveal to us your purpose
for leading this "child" to me.

May 13. Not even two weeks passed since I came home from the retreat, yet I felt so free without all of the heaviness weighing me down like before. I couldn't believe I found the strength to do it, but I somehow let both of them, (all three of them), go. I moved on without the kids I'd loved as my own, without the questions hovering over me, without the constant search to know why.

I gave them back. God held them in his hands. I accepted I'd never know anything about them again, and I knew I could trust my God to continue to love and care for them. Our investment into their lives completed a part of our story and theirs, but now

I trusted him to provide them a family in his time.

He would not leave them as orphans. I didn't need to know how or when. I only knew he'd already prepared a future for them. I didn't need to know the answers anymore. I only needed to remember God always had and still held control.

I truly believed I'd seen the last of Julian's sweet e-mail messages. God completely surprised me when I found another priceless message now two months later.

"Do you, by chance, have any pictures of my brother and sister on your computer that you can send me?" He wanted to create a virtual photo album of the three of them online via a social networking website.

"Of course I have more pictures. I'm at work right now, but I will send them to you as soon as I get home this evening." Overwhelming emotion hit each key as I typed an immediate response.

Julian and I ended up connecting live via that same social networking website, opening up a whole new world of communication between us, bridging the huge continental gap dividing us. Still twenty-five hundred miles apart, we could finally see pictures of each other and "talk" anytime via the computer. Constant conversation followed almost daily.

Thus began our quest to get to know this "forgotten" sibling.

What a handsome boy! I loved looking through current pictures he posted of himself. I even found a picture of him wearing a sweat shirt we sent for him and Juan David at Christmas, proof that they received the box and shared the contents.

I never saw this coming. Julian and I built a unique relationship rather quickly. I heard God whisper to me, "It's not over yet. Did you not know I would complete what I began the day those two faces appeared on your computer screen?"

Each night after that, I opened my computer to input grades for school, only to end the evening with long, meaningful online conversations with the older brother of the two children I lost. Before I knew it, he took center stage in my world.

"What kind of job do you have?" He wanted to know all about my job, my class, and our family.

"I teach bilingual education. I work with second graders the same age as your sister. I have two older brothers, one that lives close by and one that lives far away in another state. My parents live kind-of far, too, in another state." I asked all about his life, and he enjoyed telling me about himself.

"I am in high school, and I will graduate in November. I also take classes at a local college to learn about the manufacturing of leather goods. I love art, and I want to study fashion design. I am seventeen years old, so I probably won't live here much longer." He had less than a year left in his orphanage until he began life on his own.

Over the following three weeks, Julian and I grew closer than ever. Each of us thanked the other for loving his siblings. He couldn't express enough how much they still loved us. He filled in gaps for me, missing pieces of the story. He also let me know about Juan David and Viviana's progress since everything fell apart, even after I finally accepted I would never know another thing about them.

The kids and I even sent simple greetings to one another once again through Julian.

"Please tell your sister I said hi and give her a hug from me." And he did.

"My brother wanted me to tell you hello for him. He misses you." Those words warmed my heart.

When I finally let them go, God gave them back to me. But now instead of two, he gave me three. Abraham's sacrifice came to my mind when God asked me to give them back to him. Now Abraham's story (Gen. 22:1-13) came to my mind again as I recalled how God gave Isaac back.

"Your full purpose in their lives has not yet been fulfilled. I am not finished with this story. Keep holding on, my dear child."

Now God gave me a chance to finally get it all out, to express those things I once thought I'd never have the chance to say.

"Julian, I never got to tell your brother how sorry I am. It wasn't us. We didn't make the final decision. I never stopped loving them. I never will."

What a gift to finally let Juan David know what really happened, to tell him I still loved him. The weight of guilt I carried over the last seven months finally lifted. Their brother now communicated all those things I only wished I could have said to them once I realized I no longer had a chance.

As soon as school ended the first week of June, many long, overdue tears came spilling out of me. All of the emotions I buried deep inside during the school year and masked with busyness finally came to the surface. I didn't even know how much I really needed to cry.

Thankfully, having Julian in my life somehow made it easier. For the first time since they closed our adoption case, I finally found someone to talk to about my grief, someone from the other side who understood and knew exactly who and what I lost.

I no longer needed to wonder if they ever knew or understood what really happened. I found out Juan David knew I still tried to call after our last conversation on his birthday.

I didn't have to wonder if they thought we changed our minds about wanting to adopt them, nor did I have to wonder what they told them.

"They said you couldn't secure all the paperwork to complete the adoption." In a sense, it held truth, so I never told Julian otherwise. We secured every document but one, a final approval from Colombia. I only wanted them to know my love and prayers for them didn't stop when our communication ceased.

I hoped Julian would tell me if and when they found a family for the kids, but I never asked him to. However, when a prospective family did enter the picture that summer, he immediately let me know.

"Hey, I just wanted you to know that they found a family for my brother and sister. They call them in the evenings and come to see them on Saturdays."

Mixed emotions ran through me. Thrilled that God did indeed show me he would not leave them as orphans, it also saddened me all over again because God didn't choose us as their family.

"I am happy for them. But how do you feel about it?" Funny I didn't even consider that question when we planned on taking them away.

I'll never forget his response. "I'm happy for them. They were so excited when they found out! But I'm sad, too, because I will be alone."

"Julian, you will never be alone. We will always be a family to you." I don't know where those words even came from. Little did I know how God would hold me to that promise.

A few days later, I sat at my kitchen table with my computer open, chatting again with Julian. David and I prepared to leave the next morning for a weeklong vacation at my parent's house. I told Julian I would try my best to stay in touch while on vacation.

"I love you and miss you every day we don't connect with one another. I pray for you every day." I wanted him to know how I cherished him.

"I pray for you every day, too." His response surprised me.

"Julian, how do you know so much about God?" I truly wanted to know.

"When I still lived with my mom, a neighbor used to take both me and my brother to a Protestant church with her. We went with her every week for about a year. She also invited us to her house all the time and taught us stories from the Bible." I sure had a lot of respect for that dear neighbor. She gave those boys a solid foundation to stand on.

It finally hit me. God began to pursue a relationship with this young man at the age of nine, and he held him firmly in his grip over the last eight years. Now God brought another Christian family, our family, into his life to build upon a foundation already laid. Maybe our entire experience didn't fail, after all. Maybe our "failed" adoption actually led us straight to the "child" chosen for us, waiting for us. Straight to Julian.

With only a year left in the orphanage before living on his own as a legal adult, he needed a family to lean on for support, love, and encouragement at such a critical time in his life. God, in his sovereignty, connected us to him not long after he accepted facing the future alone.

"I'm beginning to think all of this was for you." I wrote back to Julian that evening.

"Yeah, I've been thinking the same thing." We both saw it. His response warmed my heart.

I still had a reason to sing. Hope lived inside me again. When I stopped asking why and demanding God give me answers, he showed me a purpose I couldn't see. Now this story held more than I ever imagined. How did we miss and not even consider the needs of this sibling as we pursued adopting the other two? So intent to bring them home, we didn't even really think about him and how losing his brother and sister might affect him.

Just because you've passed the allowable age for international adoption doesn't mean you don't need a family for company and support. He cried out for one as desperately as his siblings did, if not more.

"When I was younger, I always hoped a family would adopt me. I'm too old now. I just want my brother and sister to be adopted while they're still young." He gave up hoping for a family for himself, accepting he faced the future alone. I can't imagine having to feel that way, so totally alone in the world. No wonder he clung to our virtual relationship so tightly after the first time I told him I loved him.

Now we faced a new problem. He lived in Colombia. We lived in the United States. In order to have a future with this boy, we had to make it to Colombia because his status as an orphan severely limited his chances of ever coming here.

As I boarded the plane the next morning to fly to my parents' house for a week, a new song took shape inside me. While David occupied himself with the toys and books in his backpack during the flight, I started to write.

"Take us to Colombia, God." I knew we needed to keep quiet about our relationship with Julian because the adoption committee in Colombia already asked us to break our ties with his siblings. We didn't think they would react well to our involvement in their brother's life, so we agreed to keep quiet until he turned eighteen, only ten months away.

After only a month of this new communication with Julian, we agreed as a family to go see him once he turned eighteen. We felt compelled to meet him and support him as he took those first steps on his own. God has impeccable timing.

This new turn of events excited me, filling me with purpose and passion again. When David and I arrived at my parents' house, he didn't even give me a chance to fill them in. He quickly blurted out, "Next summer, we're going on our own little mission trip to Colombia to help Julian."

How we'd work out the details remained a mystery, but we knew, without a doubt, we had to go. Only ten months remained until Julian's eighteenth birthday, and we assumed he might still reside in his orphanage for a few more months after that. That left us nearly an entire year to listen for God's guidance. Maybe we'd actually make it to Colombia, after all, by June of 2011.

We made him no promises. We said we wanted to support him when he turned eighteen either by helping him further his education in some way or by helping him out with his daily needs. However, a new thought brewed inside me. I wondered if maybe God held more for us in Colombia than just Julian. He used Juan David and Viviana to burden our hearts for Colombia, and now he may use Julian to actually get us there.

As Julian and I grew closer in those summer months, I learned more about him every day. I also learned more about the traumatic life of an orphan. You always hear the stories about adoption, but how often do we hear the stories about those that never get adopted and step into the world alone? How often do we take the time to listen to those voices? Julian displayed the heart of a wounded child. He shared the hurts in his life openly with me, thanking me many times for caring so much about him.

"I love you so, so much." My heart healed a little bit more every time he typed those words to me, bonding us for life.

God set me on a new mission to prove to Julian he did not forget or abandon him. God still prepared a future for him, as well as for his siblings. I shared that message with him as often and frequently as possible.

In addition to giving me Julian to help me heal, God also gave me the opportunity to finally dive into a ministry that burned in my heart for years. I poured myself into teaching my first ladies' Bible study at my church over the summer. God planted the desire in my heart earlier, but he used me even more effectively now as a broken vessel. His light shines much brighter through our cracks and broken pieces than it does through our well-manicured, seemingly perfect lives.

When I received the list of available studies to teach from the church, God quickly made it clear which study he wanted me to teach. No book or study ever changed me like Stormie Omartian's study on The Power of a Praying Wife[2] three years earlier.

After moving to Texas several years prior with a broken marriage and a bitter heart, I took a friend's suggestion to read Stormie Omartian's book. Rather than just reading it, I prayed one of the prayers over my husband every single day until it became a habit. Through that exercise, God changed me in so many ways, and I found a life of prayer I only ever dreamed of having.

I also began to pray similar prayers over my son, my family, my leaders, and my friends on a daily basis. I learned to pray scripture, and I found an indescribable intimacy with Christ. I literally felt my heart soften toward my husband. Our marriage started to change. He began to change, and the entire climate of our home changed. Now three years later, I knew God wanted me to not only teach the study but to transparently show the ladies how he used it to change my life, to change me.

I count that teaching experience as one of the greatest blessings God ever gave me, healing my broken heart even more, giving me the joy I so desperately prayed to find again. I watched a group of strangers from different services, classes, age groups, (and even churches) assume the role of a prayer warrior for each other and for their husbands. They opened up to one another on deep levels, often shedding many unexpected tears. I can't thank God enough for what he did among those women, while healing my heart at the same time. He continued to replace my despair with incredible hope.

For the first time ever, I shared my poetry with others by printing out some of my poems each week for the ladies in the study. They encouraged me to share it more often, showing me how my poems ministered and spoke to them.

"Rachelle, my adult daughter has struggled through so many issues in her life, and she said your poetry really uplifts her. She'd like your permission to share it with her friends." My friend's request encouraged me to see that now God used my poetry, my songs, to speak life into others. They didn't share my story, but they shared my despair and wanted to claim my Hope.

"My child, it's time to stop hiding who you are and who I made you." God spoke to me deeply that summer as he used the broken pieces of my life to mold me into the person he created me to become. He used that group of women to break me out my shell of insecurity, to finally help me let the walls come down. Those women will forever occupy a special place in my heart.

Despite all the healing and renewed hope that summer, more heartache loomed on the horizon. Julian's latest news devastated me all over again.

"Rachelle, I'm so heartbroken. The family that wanted my brother and sister decided to just take Juan David, not Viviana. They want a child that can do things independently, and Viviana needs too much help and attention." It looked like Juan David and Viviana faced a permanent separation from each other. Juan David's soccer interests made him fit perfectly with the prospective family's athletic schedule. Viviana's needs claimed too much of their time.

No! This couldn't be. How could they even think about splitting them? Those two children loved each other dearly. I couldn't even fathom how God could allow this to happen after all we did to try to adopt both of them together.

"You should have seen the sadness in Viviana's eyes when she told me." Julian expressed his own deep sadness when he shared the news with me. I didn't even want to imagine how her heart broke. Not only did she not gain a family, after all, but now she watched that family tear her brother from her life.

"Julian, you need to love on her more than ever. She truly needs you now." I didn't have words to comfort him. How did I process this new devastation, anger, and confusion?

My heart hurt so much for my precious Viviana. At least she still had Julian. Maybe, I reasoned, God meant to keep her and Julian together rather than her and Juan David.

Yet my heart ached equally for Juan David. What did this news do to him? Did it break his heart? Did he feel guilty? Did the split anger him? Did he even still want an adoption without her? Did he have a choice? Could he say no?

He obviously felt happy to have a family and a future, but did his heart break to lose his beloved little sister? I doubt they ever imagined someone might separate them some day. I longed to talk with him, but I knew better than to hope for such a possibility.

I woke up one morning about a week or so later with my heart heavier than ever, aching for those two precious children. I played such a huge part of both of their lives, and now I ached to know if Juan David was okay. I looked up to God in tears and asked for one thing.

"Can I please hear from Juan David again someday?" I tearfully pleaded.

I knew a phone call would never happen. I'd never hear that boy's voice again. I knew he couldn't send me a letter. But I also knew he had my e-mail address, and I wondered if, one day, he might pull it out again and write to me. Maybe he'd write to let me know he had a family once they completed his adoption.

I would have given anything to hear from him again. Eight months already passed since the last time I shared a phone call with him. I knew I'd made quite a bold request God would likely never grant me, but I also knew he held the power to make it happen.

About a week or so later, I sat in the kitchen again with my little pink laptop open so I could chat online with Julian.

"My brother wrote you a letter over the weekend." Julian had no idea the significance of what he just said.

What? Did I read that right? "Who wrote a letter?" I asked.

"Juan David wrote a letter."

"Who did you say he wrote a letter to?"

"To you!" He replied, oblivious to the sudden, unexpected whirlwind of emotion on my end.

My eyes filled with tears. I couldn't believe it! I experienced one of those transcendent moments when you can almost feel God reaching his hand down from Heaven and touching you. He heard my cry, and he answered me. Not a soul knew I asked God to let me hear from Juan David again.

"Your words make me want to cry, Julian."

"I don't understand. I didn't say anything sad."

"God just used you to show me that he answered my prayer." I proceeded to explain my conversation with God a week earlier, believing in my heart he would not grant my request, considering the circumstances.

Wow. What a humbling moment. God showed up at my kitchen table that day. He sat with me and met me on an incredibly personal level, looking me in the eye and wiping my tears away. "I'm here, my child. I heard your cries. I saw your tears. I did not forget even one of them."

Julian took a picture of the letter to send to me via e-mail. They also took other pictures he wanted to send me, including one of him and Viviana. It didn't matter if I ever got that letter. God gave me a gift by letting me know Juan David actually wrote to me.

God heard me. He saw me. He showed himself fully present with me and fully present with those kids.

Like manna from Heaven, the simple knowledge of that letter sustained me, meeting me right at my point of need. I don't know how much more personal God could have been to me in that moment, marking a huge turning point in my faith.

God proceeded to restore us. Little by little, he revealed glimpses of how he redeemed our story. We learned what it really meant to walk by faith.

I came home a few days later from the bookstore with a new book, Sheila Walsh's Extraordinary Faith[3]. I devoured it, marking up every other page along the way. She reminded me throughout the book that faith doesn't just trust the answers will come someday. It trusts God whether we ever get answers or not. Faith doesn't mean everything will all work out in the end. No matter what news we get, God will never abandon us or leave our side. Faith trusts in the security and constant presence of a Savior. We still hurt, but in the midst of the hurt, enough grace comes each day to get us through.

I believed I possessed strong faith throughout the entire adoption process and later through the appeal. I see now I had it all wrong. I finally understand what it means to live by faith and to experience the grace that holds me together each day.

EXPERIENCING HIS GRACE

"Let us then approach the throne of grace with confidence, so that we may receive mercy and find grace to help us in our time of need." Hebrews 4:11

Surprised by Grace

Just when I thought the curtain
finally closed on the show,
when I thought I said good-bye,
accepting there'd be things I'd never know …

I put them in your hands
when you said, "Let them go, dear one,
trust me fully with this sacrifice
so I can finish what I have begun.

Then your grace appeared,
and you gave me new eyes to see
more of the work you've been doing
in the almost forgotten child number three.

I didn't see it coming,
or know he, too, needed me
to daily say I love him,
and pray for him faithfully.

I didn't see the difference
God wanted me to make in his life,
nor of the hope I could give him
to work through his internal strife.

I didn't have any clue
the hope and healing he'd give to me
through pictures and acts of gratitude
for loving his family.

Still orphans they remain today,
still brokenhearted I am,
yet confident God still works
to finish what he began.

I won't cease to intercede for them.
I will carry them daily in prayer.
I trust their Father completely
and know they're safe within his care.

I long for the day to come
when I meet that third child face to face,
yet I know I can't even fathom
how God will surprise me by grace.

Grace. A word I never understood. I even graduated from a college called Grace, and I still didn't get it. You have to experience grace to grasp it. I knew his grace would be sufficient, but I didn't know what that meant. I had to live by it day after day to understand.

God's grace came to us in many ways. It arrived in the form of an e-mail, connecting me to someone I could finally talk to, someone who understood precisely what and who I lost, who could fill in the gaps like no one else could. Grace came through comfort from friends who carried us in prayer. It came in the form of a letter from someone I thought I'd never hear from again. It came in the form of a picture, one of my sweet boy blowing me kisses and one of my precious girl smiling from ear to ear, with her hair all grown out. It also came in the form of a smile, one of the most beautiful smiles I had ever seen, on the face of a boy I wondered if I'd ever have a chance to meet.

I finally got my letter from Juan David (or the picture of it that Julian e-mailed me). What a gift! Short and sweet, he sent his love and concern for David over a recent injury. He also expressed happiness over having a family.

Julian attached pictures of the three kids, now two years older than the last time I saw them. A picture of Viviana standing with her friends showed her hair now much longer. She smiled from ear to ear, looking as pretty as ever. Another picture with Julian beside her captured the endearing love between them. Julian's smile melted my heart, one of the most beautiful smiles I've ever seen. He even attached pictures of him and Juan David together, too.

I found one particular picture of Juan David a little too blurry to see clearly.

"What is Juan David doing in that picture?" I asked Julian a few days later.

"Blowing you kisses. We took that picture just for you." Eight months of silence, and now I got kisses all the way from Colombia right to my computer screen. More than enough grace to get me through the day, especially considering I thought I'd never know another thing about him.

After months of wallowing in self-pity, I now wondered how I got so lucky to be loved by these three precious orphans. I finally found the closure I always wished for. I printed out all the pictures and hung them on the wall in the spare bedroom, surrounding a small framed poster defining scriptural faith as the substance of things hoped for, the evidence of things not seen (Hebrews 11:1).

My faith renewed even more. I started reading like crazy again. Like a sponge, I soaked up every word I could. This time, I no longer read about grief, hope, and healing. Instead, I read everything I could find on grace. I read so many unlikely stories God wrote into people's lives when they completely surrendered to him and his glory, no matter what.

Jan Winebrenner's book, *The Grace of Catastrophe—When What You Know About God Is All You Have*,[4] helped me cling to God when nothing made sense. Two other books also drew my complete attention, Bruce Wilkinson's *Dream Giver*[5] and Mark Batterson's *Wild Goose Chase*.[6] Both proved the reality that God doesn't fit in a box. Once we're willing to take him out of the box, we see how much we actually miss! In fact, as long as we keep him in the box, we might miss the whole point.

God led us on our own wild goose chase, in pursuit of his will but without a clue where it headed. We never dreamed how a seventeen-year-old Colombian orphan could turn our lives upside down. In fact, we expected to bring home a little girl from El Salvador to raise as our own only three years earlier. Our desire for a daughter led us to a little girl from Colombia, connecting us to her preteen brother, who ultimately led us to their seventeen-year-old brother.

We didn't plan it this way. We didn't envision this life. We didn't know we embarked upon this journey. But the relationship God created now between Julian and our family amazed us. God took us on the adventure of a lifetime, showing us beauty really can rise from the ashes of our losses.

Another summer almost closed again, so I used what little time remained to research any existing options for possible futures we could offer Julian. After searching for weeks, I found a program at a nearby community college offering the possibility for Julian to study in the States for a semester or two in an intensive English course already set up to help international students get their visas.

Maybe our spare bedroom belonged to Julian instead of his sister. The thought of it excited me and grew hope in me. We gave him a list of things to start acquiring to make it possible. He would gather some of the paperwork on his own, but we agreed to wait until much closer to his eighteenth birthday to talk with anyone from the orphanage about it. We still feared his social worker's and psychologist's reactions to his connection with us. At this point, we didn't know yet if God planned for Julian to come here, but it couldn't hurt to look into the possibility.

The school year soon started again, as well as my second ladies' Bible study. My first study intrigued Julian because he'd never even heard of a Bible study, so it opened up several meaningful conversations between us on the topics of scripture and prayer. Now he wanted to know more about my second study, Jennifer Rothschild's *Walking by Faith—Lessons I Learned in the Dark*.[7]

I'm the one who needed that study. As soon as I read the title, I knew God wanted me to lead it. I led my first study from personal experience, but I led this one in the dark, still walking through it. I loved walking alongside the ladies he sent to my class as they learned to dig deep in the Word. I found a passion in this area and realized I found my niche in the church, an area where I truly enjoyed serving.

As my own faith blossomed again, I watched Julian's faith grow, as well. We shared many long talks about grief, sadness, loss, and also about faith, hope, and healing. We talked often about clinging to God when it hurts and allowing him to carry us when we lose our strength. We also talked a lot about prayer. Honestly, I didn't know where he stood in his relationship with Christ, or if he even had one, but I knew God gave me this chance to plant seeds into his life. My own experience with grief helped me reach Julian in a way I never could have from a mountaintop. God showed me how my experience in the valley could help someone else.

"You know, today I kept thinking about how much God helped me throughout my life. The way you and I have gotten to know each other gives me immense happiness. To think I always believed God abandoned me, now I know that wasn't the case." Julian opened up to me in a whole new way.

"Your words right now bring me so much joy. I thought the same thing today, how God used our story of losing your siblings to ultimately change your life. Although what happened nearly destroyed us, I now see him making something beautiful I never imagined before." My reply reminded me of my final words at the women's spiritual retreat when I expressed God breaking us in order to bring about something beautiful. The joy I desperately prayed for returned. I felt it deep within.

"I thought that same thing many times. The plan of God—it's a wonderful thing. I now know God has a plan for me, and he has a plan for everyone." His response held a new hope.

"I'm so glad to hear you say that, because a few short months ago, I know you didn't think that way." I typed with incredible emotion, in awe of God's evident working.

"I know," he responded.

He got it. He got the message I poured into him, day in and day out. God did not forgot or abandon him. Reading those heartfelt words made the entire experience worth it. God used us in a mighty way to change that boy's whole mindset.

I dealt with fear every day, thinking I might lose him, too. Our connection still remained "secret." I knew I could accept the loss better than I accepted losing his siblings because at least I saw a purpose. Our relationship with him strengthened his trust in God. That alone would have given me a sense of closure if I ever needed it.

Continuing our quest to bring Julian to the States, I contacted the community college about him. A kind lady led me through all the paperwork he would need.

"I just want you to know, though, that his status as an orphan might make it difficult for him to gain a visa. I have a few suggestions of things he can do to give himself a better chance, though."

When I shared all the information with Julian, it overwhelmed him. He wanted to talk to the orphanage director first so she could help with the paperwork.

I freaked out, positive she would not react well to his connection with us. I braced myself emotionally for another huge loss. I prayed my heart out, and we waited. Several days passed, yet we heard nothing from Julian.

"We lost him." My heart felt so heavy with sadness as Mike and I discussed our assumption that our fear of losing him turned into a reality. I sure would miss him. I grew to love that boy more than I ever imagined.

By the end of the week, after yet another night in tears, I did hear from him again. He talked with the director, who cared dearly for him, and she reacted very positively regarding this possibility. She told him to talk with both his social worker and his psychologist, along with his legal defender.

Those titles alone scared me, especially the psychologist. The psychologist over our adoption case stood so firmly against our ability to parent an adoptive child. The thought of another Colombian psychologist involved again left a bitter taste in my mouth. Even in a completely different situation, my nerves went crazy while we waited on their "approval" of us.

About a week passed before Julian found a chance to talk to everyone involved, and we both breathed a huge sigh of relief when they all showed positive reactions. We no longer felt a need to keep quiet about our relationship with him. His social worker showed the only negative response from anyone, only because she wished he'd told her first. She constantly looked out for him to find him opportunities. She meticulously worked to find the best possible future for the kids who never get adopted. If an opportunity like this existed for him, she needed to know about it.

Julian gave them all my e-mail address, and they said

they would contact me. I collected all the information from the community college to give to his social worker as soon as she contacted me.

Meanwhile, our relationship with him grew by leaps and bounds now that everyone knew about it. Our love for him grew more every day, as did his love for us. We became the family he'd always dreamed of having. We also became his prayer warriors, along with our entire adult class at church. So many people prayed for him and the direction his future might take him, more than he will ever know, probably more than we ourselves will ever know. I loved him like a son, and I told him so as often as I could. When I prayed for David every morning, I prayed for him, too.

Our family kept quite busy throughout the fall. Between normal school and work hours, Mike coached David's soccer team, and I took pictures, managed the soccer website, and made photo books for the team. I continued teaching the ladies' Bible study, and we all three stayed involved in church activities. When I found a quiet moment, I devoured book after book. God filled me with an incredible hunger to know his Word and the stories of how he worked in other people's lives following unexpected tragedies. Stories of people who found the Light by walking through the dark captivated me.

It amazed me to see how close I seemed to arrive at the end of my grief, when suddenly my hope and confidence crumbled. October nearly knocked me to the ground. The day before Halloween marked a solid year since the end of our adoption pursuit. Costumes everywhere screamed insult and shame at me, reminding me of our greatest failure. So many triggers brought out emotions I didn't realize I still felt. Tears came unexpectedly at all the wrong times. Guilt crept back in to beat me up all over again.

Julian stayed busy to finish his last semester of high school (their school year ends in November), so we maintained very limited contact with him. Whenever we did communicate, he asked if anyone from the orphanage wrote to me yet, and I had to say no every time. Neither one of us knew why they stalled to contact me.

I'd done so well lately as I watched God work wonders in both our life and in Julian's, so I didn't expect to find those old tears stream down my cheeks again. Memories tormented me. Juan David's adoption process seemed to progress well with his prospective family, but he spent so much time with them that he rarely saw Viviana anymore. He stayed at the orphanage during the week and then lived with the family on the weekends, meaning he didn't spend Saturdays with his sister like before. My heart ached for her. I knew she must miss him terribly. Julian worked on the weekends, so he couldn't spend those Saturday afternoons with her either. Knowing we let her down haunted me.

I noticed my heart gradually begin to let go of Juan David. I knew another family now embraced him, so I didn't long for him or hurt for him. But I longed for his sister, and October reminded me daily that we failed her. I could barely get out of bed to face the actual day of the anniversary at the end of the month, guilt weighing me down like a heavy blanket.

Yet when November 1 came along, I felt completely different. The year passed, and a new month started, marking a new year. God did something new in me, and he faithfully filled my heart with renewed purpose. I still ached for Viviana, and I desperately prayed for a family for her. But my grieving suddenly ended. I grieved their loss for an entire year, and now I knew I could move on. By God's grace, I found both healing and restoration.

UNDERSTANDING HIS PURPOSE

For my thoughts are not your thoughts, neither are your ways my ways," declares the Lord. "As the heavens are higher than the earth, so are my ways higher than your ways and my thoughts than your thoughts.
Isaiah 55:8-9

Gaining a Son

I lay awake in bed last night
with you heavy on my mind.
I remembered how my plans changed,
while watching the last year in rewind.

I thought I lost everything
when my dream crumbled before my eyes.
My hope of mothering your siblings
came to a screeching halt after many tries.

So angry with my heavenly Father,
so hurt down to the core,
so humiliated and embarrassed,
what could it all have been for?

When I reached a point of surrender
and trusted him with them once more,
suddenly you appeared in the picture,
and I saw hope I didn't see before.

My heart caught hold of a purpose,
your presence helped me finally grieve.
I began to love you as I loved them,
and I gained a new son, I believe.

A year after everything crumbled,
after picking up the debris from the bomb,
you wrote the words that confirmed it for me,
when you started to call me "Mom."

"How are you doing today, Mom?" Julian sent me a random message during the day, but his new choice of vocabulary brought tears to my eyes when I read it.

Could God have made it more obvious that he chose Julian as our son even without allowing us to adopt him? What a pleasant surprise when he called me "Mom" in early November. The first time he wrote it, it melted my heart. I could only imagine what I meant to him now after all this time, or how long it had been since he even used that word. It solidified our bond, binding us together for life. Through it all, I gained another son.

Only a few days remained until Juan David's thirteenth birthday. Since he still resided at the orphanage during the week, I asked Julian to please wish him a happy birthday for me. Juan David got my message, and it meant the world to me that he knew I didn't forget his special day. I never imagined a year ago after our last conversation that I'd still send him a birthday greeting a year later. Truth be told, I didn't think I'd ever communicate with him again.

God filled the entire month of November with his goodness and blessing, opening several doors we didn't even know existed. I remembered one of my particularly long conversations with Julian in the summer. He mentioned how he would love to study in the States, but he also turned the table to ask, "Have you ever thought about coming to Colombia to live?"

"An opportunity like that would be a dream come true!" His question actually brewed in my mind over several months as I wondered if God had more waiting for us in Colombia than just Julian. Deep down in my heart, I believed God might call us to serve as missionaries in Colombia someday and use Julian to draw us there. I didn't know this for sure, nor did I have any clue how it could ever work out. I researched several mission boards I connected with in my college days to see if they had missionaries in Colombia, but none of them worked in Bogotá near Julian.

I brought in the mail one day that month, quickly ready to throw all the "junk mail" in the fire currently burning in the fireplace. A letter caught my eye, so I decided to look at it first. We received yearly letters during the holiday season from a certain mission organization, and, truthfully, neither of us knew how we'd gotten on the mailing list. We didn't even know anyone who served with them. As I pulled the newsletter out of the envelope that day, I wondered if any of their missionaries lived in Colombia, specifically in Bogotá.

When I realized they did have missionaries serving near Julian, I soon found myself glued to their website. The home page also contained a link to a Christian school in Bogotá run completely in English for missionary children and also for Colombian children of parents who serve in the ministry somehow. I found the jackpot, this little gold mine! I could feel my heart beat faster as I read more about the school, its mission, and personal testimonies from teachers currently working there.

Could this be that wide open door for us to get to Colombia as missionaries? I had to find out more. I contacted the mission organization to say we planned to visit Colombia in June. I asked if we could visit with the missionaries in Bogotá to observe some of the ministries going on.

Mike and I shared a passion for the mission field, after spending a summer working in Mexico together as an engaged couple, so finding a possible ministry to join in Colombia stirred my heart. We had to find out if God had a plan for us there, so we agreed to scope things out when we arrived in Colombia to meet Julian.

I now faced the upcoming holidays with joy and gratitude in my heart rather than the despair I faced a year ago. I cherished the time with my parents when they came to visit us again for Thanksgiving. My mom, David, and I hit the stores on Black Friday like we always do, but I didn't wince in pain as we walked through the toy aisles this year. The princess outfits didn't torment me as I walked by them either.

The orphanage recently gave me permission to send Julian a Christmas gift, so I thought of him this year as I shopped. He told me once that he didn't own a Bible, and I remembered saying maybe I'd send him one for Christmas. I searched through the Spanish Bibles at a local Christian bookstore to find him the perfect one. David and I worked together to find the right translation for him. We wanted a Bible with both the Old and New Testaments, but still little enough to fit inside a small box. My heart filled with joy when we made our purchase that day.

It's amazing what latching on to hope can do for you. We didn't feel like we'd reached the mountaintop yet, but we anxiously and eagerly climbed our way up. It felt good to love and be loved again.

Julian's high school graduation approached quickly, but he

ran into an unexpected problem. Since he attended a year-long course at a technical school at the same time, he did not attend his high school classes as consistently as he should have. Now with graduation right around the corner, he found out he might not graduate because he missed too many classes. The news devastated him.

It concerned us, too. Without a diploma, he couldn't take the courses we hoped for him to take here. We prayed for God to make a way for him to graduate.

Julian said he had to take a test to show how much he learned throughout high school, and, luckily, he only fell short in one area—Calculus. The school gave him remedial help and allowed him to take the test again. We prayed him through it, along with all of his prayer warriors at our church, but when he took the test the second time, he still didn't pass. So discouraged and scared, he gave it one more shot by hiring a tutor before meeting with his teacher to demonstrate what he learned. That boy had more prayers going out for him than he even knew. He finally passed, graduating a week later.

He made it, so he totally surprised me when he said he didn't even want to attend his graduation.

"Why don't you want to go? You worked so hard!" I asked.

"I don't have anyone to go with me." He invited one person from the orphanage, but she couldn't go. He didn't feel like going to his own graduation all alone. Thankfully, when he realized the orphanage already paid for his attire, he changed his mind at the last minute.

I chatted online with him that morning while he got ready. "I would have loved to go with you if I were there."

"I know. Thank you." He nervously put on his cap and gown, saying he looked like a penguin. I loved being able to "spend" the morning with him.

He did meet up with a female friend at his graduation, one who also grew up in the orphanage with him but no longer lived there. He didn't take any pictures, but she did, and he sent those to me. I immediately printed them out to hang on the wall in the spare bedroom. He sure made a handsome graduate, making me one proud "Mom."

Months earlier I made a small photo book with pictures of Julian and his siblings. He never found an opportunity to get a picture of the three of them together, despite my begging, so the book only contained pictures of him and Juan David together or him and Viviana together. Now that I had graduation pictures, I taped them onto the inside and outside back cover of the little book. I bought a CD of one of his favorite songs, and I carefully packed it all together in the little box with his new Bible.

His Christmas package still felt incomplete, but an idea came to my mind about what it lacked. When I sent Juan David that little Texas keychain over a year ago, I bought myself a matching one as a keepsake. Juan David now had a new family to love him, although they still hadn't adopted him, and my heart let him go. I wanted to give Julian the matching one rather than keep it for myself. He and Juan David could share a common possession, plus now it could remind Julian of a family in Texas that loved him as their son, now his family forever. We didn't need adoption papers to declare it true this time around.

We just turned the calendar to December, but I couldn't wait to send Julian's gift. That little box seemed ready to "bust at the seams" because it held so much love within it. I couldn't bear for it to sit on my counter when it could be in his hands. I carefully wrapped it all up tight, drove to the Mail Mart, and sent it off.

What an odd feeling, walking into that Mail Mart, again with yet another package to send to that same orphanage in Colombia, another one of those moments I never could have imagined taking place. Our story touched the owner of the Mail Mart so much that she gave us a discount for every package we mailed those kids. Now, a year later, she recognized me as soon as I walked in the door and gave me the discount again.

I secured the tracking numbers for my package and watched

online almost every hour until that little box reached its destination.

"Mil gracias. (Thanks a million!) The gift is beautiful. I love you guys so much. I don't need to receive another gift at all for Christmas. This is more than enough." Julian thanked me immediately for the gift.

To add to the excitement, the same day I put the package in the mail, the director of the orphanage also gave me permission to start making phone calls to Julian. I only ever heard his voice once, and I didn't even remember what it sounded like during those brief moments of a conversation Juan David arranged over a year ago.

Amidst all the hustle and bustle of Julian's graduation, Thanksgiving, the Christmas season, finishing up the first semester at school, and sending Julian his gift, apparently a lot of activity went on behind the scenes in Colombia, too. His social worker found him an opportunity to continue his studies in Bogotá, which explained why she never contacted me.

It disappointed me to know he wouldn't come to stay with us, but this opportunity thrilled me. The program we wanted to get him in here only served as a stepping stone without any clear leading. His social worker found him an opportunity to study the Arts, his main passion. So, we dropped our pursuit to bring him here and went back to Plan A, to support him in furthering his studies once he exited government care.

I thought back to that lonely boy I barely knew at the beginning of the summer, the boy who felt so alone, completely forgotten about by God. God now flooded him with more love and opportunities for his future than he ever dreamed. It honored and humbled us to play a role in his story.

I spent Christmas Eve with half of my heart in Colombia once again. (Perhaps it never left.) I researched airline prices for our upcoming trip in June and couldn't believe the prices we found, hundreds of dollars cheaper per ticket than we expected! When our friends who travel often saw the prices, they suggested we book those tickets immediately. Mike hurried to get his vacation time approved for the following summer, and we booked them!

This was real. We finally had tickets to take us to Colombia.

It felt surreal after everything that led us to this point. I gave Julian the dates, but he didn't have any idea where he would be or what he might be doing at that time. We'd arrive almost two months after his eighteenth birthday, so he didn't know if he'd still reside in government care or live on his own by then. We felt confident God told us to go in June, so it forced us to take a huge step of faith.

I think I glowed on Christmas Day. What a year, filled with a whirlwind of emotions, leaving us committed to and smitten by this seventeen-year-old boy in an orphanage in Colombia. Not just any seventeen-year-old boy from any random orphanage, but the sibling of the two children we failed to adopt, living in the same orphanage I called so often in the previous year. God indeed redeemed our story by giving us Julian, our Christmas miracle.

"Hi. May I please speak with Julian?" I could hardly believe I dialed the number to that same orphanage again, now over a year later.

"Hello? This is Julian speaking." I barely recognized his voice.

"Merry Christmas, Julian! It's me, Rachelle!" I don't think he recognized my voice either on the other end of the line.

"Hi, Rachelle! It's so good to hear you." His voice held gratitude for my call. After all the times he watched his brother and sister receive my phone calls, now he held the phone on the other end of the line as the recipient.

Oh, to hear his voice again. I adored that boy. The pieces fit together now, and the puzzle started to make sense, despite all the times I asked God, "Why Colombia? Why that orphanage? Why those two kids?"

Each piece mattered.

I signed up to teach another Bible study in January, Beth Moore's study on John, *The Beloved Disciple*.[8] It amazed me how well I related with the characters surrounding Jesus' life and crucifixion. They, too, went through a whirlwind of emotions, watching Jesus gain momentum, draw more and more followers, only to be captured and crucified before their eyes. They struggled with their doubts, wondering if they had mistaken the reality of Jesus and why they should follow him. Yet witnessing his resurrection convinced them to tell as many people as possible about the reality of Christ.

When our adoption pursuit ended in "death," God brought about a resurrection of hope with Julian. We watched God do amazing things for all of us, and I couldn't keep my mouth shut about him. My hunger and passion for the Word consumed me, and I poured my heart into teaching Bible studies and guiding others into scripture. The more intimately I knew Christ, the more I wanted others to know him that way, too.

UNDERSTANDING HIS PLAN

*Delight yourself in the Lord and he will give you
the desires of your heart.
Psalm 37:4*

The Picture We Didn't See

I'll never forget those fourteen pictures
that brought your brother and sister to me,
the way they captured my heart,
as if there were only two I could see.

The other twelve filled a background,
so for those two I began to pray.
A desire to meet them grew strong,
we soon were on our way.

Things fell into place,
so naturally it seemed.
Our calling so certain
as we lived out our dream.

No one had a clue
God had other plans in mind.
The path he led us on,
now just about to wind.

After months of reexamining
and asking where we missed a turn,
we found you stranded on the highway,
so lost and lonely we'd soon learn.

We gave you hope you didn't believe in,
a love you didn't know.
We encourage you daily to turn to Jesus
to lift you when you're low.

Today I remembered those pictures,
and now I am keenly aware
he drew my heart to your siblings' photos
because YOUR picture … wasn't there.

The New Year always has a tendency to get you to reflect over everything you experienced in the previous year. What were the highlights or the lows? Did you experience unforgettable moments, milestones, or hard things to swallow? What lessons did you learn? Did you have any huge revelations or ah-ha moments that left you standing speechless?

I began this New Year in awe of God turning our tragedy into a story of hope. I looked back and saw his fingerprints all over this last year of our life. How could I even begin to think of shutting up now? I couldn't wait to start my next Bible study.

"Father, help me to communicate transparently enough with these ladies so you can speak boldly through me." I wanted them to see Christ, not me.

The first assignment in the study led us each to write a letter to God, expressing the desires of our heart. I gave it a lot of thought and prayer before I started to write.

> God,
>
> On the last morning of the retreat, she approached me, handed me my prayer bell and told me you led her to pray for me to receive the desires of my heart. I still remember how the tears immediately welled up in my eyes and began to fall—the first tears I cried all weekend.
>
> Fully convinced you asked me to give the desires of my heart back to you that weekend and trust you to take care of them, her words caught me off guard. You asked me to put my precious treasures back in your hands, just as you asked Abraham to sacrifice his son, the greatest desire of his heart.
>
> So when she said those words, I didn't understand what they meant. At that moment, I desired nothing more than to still bring the kids home, but I knew it wouldn't happen because you just asked me to let them go. I came home with the assurance that I would receive the desires of my heart, but I no longer knew what those desires were.
>
> I'd long given up on my hope of serving in missions, I didn't even have the slightest desire to conceive another child, and the thought of pursuing another adoption remained out of the question. They had my heart. So I've been on a quest over the last year to figure out exactly what my heart even still desired after all of this.
>
> Now in retrospect, I see. You gave me new desires. I wanted to know more, anything at all, about Juan David and Viviana (even though I accepted that weekend I likely never would). I hoped to grow again in my faith, to find that intimacy with you like before. I wanted to involve ourselves heavily

in ministry and to see a purpose for all that we suffered.

Now I can see you began by giving me a precious gift, a precious soul who became my "son" over the following year. You gave me Julian, and in doing so, you satisfied the desire of my heart to know more about Juan David and Viviana and how their life continued. You gave me closure with Juan David, eight months after my last phone call with him.

You gave me a new hope of missions and connected me with missionaries in Colombia I'd never even met before. You presented me opportunities to lead women's Bible studies at Lake Pointe Church, each time bringing new relationships in my life to help me heal.

You taught me so much more about your character, and you drew me into a more intimate relationship with you than I'd ever known. Through my pain and my broken heart, you held me together, carried me through each day when I had no strength left to stand, and became my ultimate Sustainer. You slowly healed me one day at a time, restored my brokenness, gave me a new purpose, and filled my heart with joy once again.

Today, I again wonder what my heart truly desires. First and foremost, I want to see Julian give his life wholeheartedly to you. I want to meet him and be a godly mother figure to him for as long as he needs me. I want to stay connected to him for many years to come. I want to continue to grow closer to him, and I want the moment we meet to represent one of the most memorable moments of both of our lives.

I want to find a ministry to work with in Colombia—one we will come back to year after year or one we will eventually join full time. I want to see our story come full circle so others cannot deny you have been at work all along, and they will see that only you could have orchestrated and authored a story like ours.

I want to publish my poetry. I want to write a book, to write full time about your awesome power and presence. I want to inspire others to dive into your Word and to represent your reality to others because they see you so clearly in me.

I hope for all of these opportunities. But God, more than anything else, I want my precious Viviana to be adopted into a Christian home where someone will teach her to love you deeply. I, of course, still want nothing more than to bring her home, to raise her myself. But to know she has a Christian mommy who loves you and will teach her to love you is my heart's greatest desire.

Thank you for giving me the desires of my heart.

Your beloved daughter,
Rachelle (Jan. 9, 2011)

Over the following six months, I stood back in awe while God let me check off almost every item on my "list" as he granted me each desire. Deep down in my heart, I hoped for another chance to adopt Viviana if the committee did not match her with a family by the time we made it to Colombia. I prayed for her day and night, while she and I sent sweet messages to one another through Julian.

Yet one more bittersweet moment remained. Be careful when you ask God to grant you the desires of your heart because he may do so more quickly than you think or even want.

"They found a mother for Viviana. She's coming to adopt her in two weeks, on February 7." Julian struggled to tell me the news, overjoyed and relieved for his sister, though heartbroken himself. Not even a month had passed since I wrote my letter to God expressing my desire for her adoption. Before anyone even had time to process what happened, she moved to Europe to begin her new life.

My princess finally had a mommy of her own. Julian and I felt thrilled for her, but my heart broke to lose her again, and it crushed Julian to finally have to let go of his beautiful little sister.

They told him she could contact him once she had enough time to bond well with her mother. Who knew how long that might take?

I found Julian online the day before Viviana left, a couple hours before my normal time to call. He planned to see her one more time that evening, so I asked if he wanted me to call on a different day.

"No. I am so sad today. I need to hear your voice." We prayed together so faithfully for her to gain a family. Yet when God answered our prayers, Julian wasn't ready to let her go (not that a sibling should ever have to let another sibling go).

The following morning, she skipped out of his life, out of all of our lives.

"Mommy, will she still love us?" David asked me during dinner one evening that same week.

"Of course, she will, David." I answered, glad to know he tried to process this event.

Mike then asked him, "Do you still love her?"

He said he did, and we all agreed we would never stop loving her. She would forever have our hearts.

Now the middle of February, we had four months left until our trip to Colombia. Other than Julian and Juan David, we didn't know a soul there. Well, we knew the man who previously pastored our Spanish congregation at church who recently moved back to Bogotá. However, I had not been able to get in touch with him, despite many repeated tries.

I still can't believe we planned a trip to a foreign country we'd never been to in hopes of meeting a boy we'd never seen before except in pictures. We didn't know anyone, we had no idea where to stay, how to get around, what it might cost us, or even what to do while there. We didn't even know for sure if we could see Julian. But, we booked our flights and blocked out fifteen days of our year to spend there.

We did contact one missionary, who tried to put us in touch with another missionary, so that might cover a few days of our time.

I thought back to the Christian school I found online back in November. We couldn't make it all the way to Colombia and not at least visit the school.

I found the director's contact information on the webpage, and I sent her an e-mail explaining the story leading us to Colombia. I also explained our desire to scope out the mission field in order to find out if God might have a ministry for us in Colombia. I told her I had a degree in Christian ministries as well as teaching experience in bilingual education, so I asked if we could see the school and perhaps talk to a few teachers during those two weeks in June.

When she responded back to me a few weeks later, she seemed enthusiastic to meet us. Our story touched her. We'd arrive in time for graduation, and several teachers would be coming and going through the school the following week.

Wow. God began to show me his perfect timing. My teaching experience and background interested her, and she hoped Mike might consider joining the maintenance team at the school, as well. Her next question still brings me goose bumps.

"Will you need a place to stay?" She explained that many of her teachers live there as missionaries and go back to the States right after graduation. We could stay in one of their apartments for a minimal cost, helping them out financially in their absence.

I could hardly believe it. Four months away and still clueless about any details of our trip, God connected us with yet another ministry to visit and also gave us a place to stay. Plus, we'd get to help another missionary by staying there. Only in God's economy do things like this ever happen. What a confirmation that we heard God's guidance correctly even regarding the dates of this trip.

We still had no idea where Julian might reside or where he'd work, but God showed me he walked far ahead of us in every aspect of our story. He kept tapping my shoulder, whispering in my ear, "This is one trip I'm not letting you plan. I already planned every moment of every day for you."

Before I knew it, Julian's eighteenth birthday arrived, another bittersweet day. He finally entered adulthood, but that also meant huge changes, including a loss of the only security he ever knew. He didn't have any idea how much longer he could stay in government care, and his social worker had not even secured his college possibility yet.

After finishing his technical school in November, he worked full time as an apprentice in the area he studied, Manufacturing of Leather Goods. He worked for a famous purse retailer, making high quality, expensive leather purses in a factory. He embraced the experience and learned a lot of responsibility, but it made him long to study even more in order to do something more suited to his actual artistic skills. His ambitious attitude made me proud, never settling for less than he desired. Now only seven weeks separated us from finally meeting face to face.

Time flew after that point. As each day brought us closer to boarding a plane to Colombia, I struggled with a variety of mixed emotions. So ready to meet Julian, I constantly envisioned our first moment together. I could hardly wait to give him that first hug, look into his eyes, and say, "I'm here. We're finally here. We made it."

Yet the fact he still knew nothing about where he would be made me more nervous every day. Would he still live in the orphanage? Would they let him leave to see us? Would we have permission to go there, considering Juan David still resided there on weekdays as he continued to await his final adoption?

Some days I panicked and wondered if we'd make it to Colombia at all—and perhaps not even get to see Julian after all we'd planned. Would our trip even include him? Or would we visit the two ministries we contacted and then spend our vacation exploring a new country as a family of three? I knew deep in my heart God walked way ahead of us, but anxiety still tormented me. Only a few weeks till our departure, yet I knew we'd gotten this close to leaving for Colombia before. Anything could still go wrong.

Despite my anxiety, God orchestrated every detail. Someone from the school contacted me with the exact address of the apartment we planned to stay in, and they arranged for a driver to take us there from the airport. Plus they told us the exact amount to rent the apartment for two weeks, freeing us to create some sort of budget.

A repeated conversation with David came to my mind.

"I can't believe how much money we lost in that adoption process." Anger gripped his little heart for quite a while.

"God will bless us. Someday, somehow, He will bless us." I had no other response to give him.

Now we watched God pour out his blessings by providing a furnished apartment for us at only a fraction of the cost of a hotel.

As each remaining day passed by more quickly, a new fear arose inside me. If time flew this fast now, would it fly just as fast while there? If we indeed got to spend time with Julian, I hoped each day would creep by us so we could savor every moment. I fought constant anxiety during those final weeks.

Fighting Fear

What is it that awaits us
now only fifteen days away,
at the tip of South America,
where I find my thoughts each day?

As each one passes by me,
my heart skips another beat.
I can't help but hold my breath …
Could this dream, too, end in defeat?

Am I claiming wishful thinking,
or a hope only God can give?
Am I safe to claim his guidance?
Is it alright to let hope live?

Just what awaits us in Colombia?
What could your purpose be?
As we take this giant step by faith,
please give us eyes to see…

A teaching job, a ministry,
an organization to support,
or could it be a doorway
back to a dream cut short?

So many possibilities
might await us there.
My heart spins in circles,
as I pour it out to God in prayer.

Take away these anxious feelings.
Take away this trembling fear.
May every step we take
be filled with peace that you are near.

HOPING

for a different end this time …

Months away was all it seemed,
before the months soon turned to weeks.
When the weeks turned into days …
All my emotion reached its peak!

Only days till I could hold them,
only days till our eyes would meet,
till those days unexpectedly vanished,
all the waiting a useless feat.

How our hearts were broken,
how shattered I was inside,
I'd never hold them in my arms,
All our dreams had died.

Now here I sit again,
watching months turn into weeks.
I failed to guard my heart.
Only hope is what I seek.

Hope that one day soon we'll meet,
one day soon we will embrace.
Everything we all have suffered
will finally be replaced with grace.

Yet as each week passes by me,
as our day comes nearer still,
I find myself in fear again,
the thought gives me a chill.

What if something happens?
What if, by chance, you're sent away?
What if we finally make it there,
and never get our meeting day?

Yet still I hope amidst my fear
God won't take you away,
one day soon I'll really meet you,
"this child for whom I prayed."

No matter what future awaits us,
I know now after such intense prayer
God has a plan for us in Colombia,
and he used you to take us there.

I Samuel 1:27

I prayed for this child, and the Lord has granted me what I asked of him.

Fear. Anxiety. Excitement. Hope. So many mixed emotions competed for my attention. Yet some days, I felt nothing at all. Maybe I subconsciously guarded my heart because too many emotions overwhelmed me. I feared letting my expectations get set too high.

On the other hand, I purposely didn't let myself set any expectations because I knew God's plans always trumped mine. I didn't want to miss whatever he had waiting for us because he had a tendency to blow us away.

Now with our flight only days away, the time arrived to find out if, when, and where we could meet Julian. He still lived in the orphanage. He did not start any classes yet, nor did he find a new job. Since the first time we met online, he constantly ran in at least five directions at once. Now his calendar remained empty without a single commitment.

I wrote a letter via e-mail to the orphanage director to request approval for him to leave the orphanage to spend time with us. In my letter, I explained our connection to Julian first. Then I explained our purpose and length of stay in Bogotá.

"We would like to spend as much time with Julian as you will allow us. He is more than welcome to stay with us the entire two weeks, or we can take him back to the orphanage in the evenings if you would prefer. We would like to support Julian in some way as he enters this next stage of his life. Please let us know the best way to help him."

Her response overwhelmed me. Not only did she give permission for Julian to stay with us, as part of our family, for the entire duration of our trip, but she wanted to arrange a meeting for us to discuss his future needs with his psychologist and social worker.

"I think it's wonderful for Julian to finally have the support of a family." Wow. She already called us his family.

I fretted over finding our way around the city without a guide, and now, we would have a native Colombian with us at all times. I worried about the possibility of not getting to see Julian, and now we'd get him for fourteen days and nights straight. I thought we might not even step foot in the orphanage, and now we had a meeting scheduled there with the very titles of people that terrified me, the very same psychologist and social worker that Juan David and Viviana shared. These details thrilled me, sent me beyond excited, yet scared me all over again, especially regarding that meeting.

Thankfully, our prayer warriors covered us in prayer that last week before we left. While many of our friends and acquaintances thought us crazy to even go, those closest to us knew God planned to do something huge with our family. We didn't just plan a random trip over the last six months. God prepared us for this trip over a three-year period, leading us on a painful journey of faith in preparation for how our lives would change over these fifteen days in Colombia. He walked so far ahead of us. We had no idea.

Our last few days sped by us until we finally boarded that plane early Saturday morning, June 4, 2011. I don't remember a bit of our long awaited flight. Before I knew it, my little boy exclaimed, "I can't believe it! We're here! We're actually here! We're really in Colombia!"

We made it. Our flight landed, and our driver picked us up right on time. After a long drive through the streets of Bogotá, we arrived at a beautiful apartment complex. Upon our arrival, we found ourselves in the middle of a communication gap, one that divinely left us stranded on the doorstep of an unexpected friend, Clarita. To be honest, she didn't look too thrilled to entertain strangers on a cold, wet day, but two weeks later she admitted her gratitude to God for dropping us off on her doorstep.

No one could find the only people in the complex with the keys to our apartment, so we spent a few hours with Clarita, one of the apartment owners' good friends. She also lived in Colombia as a missionary but no longer worked for the Christian school. Since she didn't work for the school, we never would have had a reason to meet her, making this "accidental" appointment even more divine. She graciously let us use her computer to let our families know we made it to Colombia safely, and then we used her phone to call Julian.

"We're here, Julian! We made it!" I finally got to say the words, but we still lacked that first embrace.

"Wow. You sound soooo close!!!" I'll never forget the emotion in his voice.

"We will come to get you tomorrow morning at ten o'clock."

"Okay. I will wait outside for you." Not even twenty-four hours remained until we could finally meet.

Clarita took us to get some cash out at the ATM, and she walked us to a pizza place to have dinner, the first we'd eaten since two o'clock that morning. Already almost four o'clock in the afternoon, the long day began to hit us. While we ate, she inquired a lot about what brought us to Colombia. After we explained the whole story, she offered to accompany us to the orphanage the next morning to get Julian.

Hmmm. Did God provide for yet another detail? Scratch out our fear of taking a taxi by ourselves in this very foreign country.

Finally, the keys showed up, and we had a chance to get into our apartment to relax, unpack, and regroup. Then it hit us—we physically stood in Colombia, after all this time. Our lives would change forever the next morning when we met our "son" face to face.

UNITED AT LAST

"For I know the plans I have for you," declares the Lord, "plans to prosper you and not to harm you, plans to give you hope and a future."
Jeremiah 29:11

Who Could Have Imagined?

The kids had all been chosen,
carefully selected to participate
in a summer full of adventures,
scattered all over the United States.

Each child came with a story,
some of abandonment, neglect, or abuse,
but they all came in search of a family.
What more did they have to lose?

Though your own time already passed,
too old to be chosen to come,
you bravely sent off your siblings.
I'm sure your heart went numb.

You were convinced they'd join a family,
and your dreams for them would come true,
but who in the world could have imagined
they instead found a family for you?

God's ways are so mysterious,
and sometimes hurt more than I can say,
but now that I have you as my son,
I wouldn't want it any other way.

We made it to the orphanage Sunday morning right around ten o'clock. We called before we left, so Julian anxiously waited for us. What incredible emotion overcame me as we drove down the street he lived on, the same streets I saw in someone else's adoption video online, streets I assumed I'd never have the chance to see. The taxi driver dropped us off in front of the house at the specific address Julian gave me.

He said he'd wait outside, but the boy sitting outside didn't look like him, so we proceeded to the door. I feared not recognizing him even after seeing his pictures. Several boys his age stood gathered around as we walked in the door. It didn't take long for my eyes to meet with Julian's. I recognized those eyes in an instant. Without saying a word, I reached my arms around his neck and hugged him.

The rest of those first few moments remain a blur. I know he met Mike and David, and we introduced him to our new friend, Clarita, who accompanied us. Julian introduced us to the director and one of his house parents, and then he disappeared to go get the key.

"It's so good for Julian to finally get to know you in person. You already obviously know each other well, but I know how much it means to him to finally meet you." The director and I talked while I waited for Julian to come back, and I saw for myself how dearly she cared for him.

Julian returned after a few minutes, and then he gave us a quick tour of his house. It felt like one of those out-of-body experiences, so unfortunately, I didn't take it all in like I wanted to. Emotion overwhelmed me. Thankfully, Mike snapped picture after picture.

I do remember seeing the bedroom Julian shared with five other boys, the specific bunk he slept on in the corner of the room, and another little room with the only computer in the house—the exact place where he spent hour upon hour in the evenings "talking" to me via a keyboard over the last year and a half. He also introduced us to the one boy in the house he considered a friend, and then we started to leave.

"We can give you a tour of the entire orphanage when you come back on Tuesday for our meeting. I can show you the house where Viviana lived." The director's comment made me realize they respected the relationship I built with Viviana. She didn't mention Juan David, but Julian already warned me we couldn't see him because it would be too difficult for him emotionally. I understood and did not want to cause any problems with his new family in the process of adopting him. Still, I wondered what he thought about us finally being there, only this time to meet his brother. I promised him I'd come, and God let me fulfill my promise, though for different reasons now.

As we walked out the door, Clarita said her good-byes, as well, and the director mentioned seeing her again in two days for our meeting. A different missionary we contacted planned to accompany us to our meeting, so I explained that Clarita would not return with us on Tuesday. The director hesitated for a moment and then offered to give us all a tour of the orphanage right then. She gave Julian permission to take us through all of the homes, so we followed him into each of the six houses. We saw both of the homes where Viviana lived and grew up, and we met her house parents and likely her friends.

Our tour ended with Juan David's home. He spent the weekend with his new family, but we met all of his friends and housemates and saw where he ate, played, and slept. It felt strange to know he still lived there, and we actually stood in his home.

My gaze locked immediately on the phone hanging on the wall right outside the kitchen where he told me it had been. I stared at that phone, suddenly reliving so many of our conversations. I could still hear all the noise, the pots and pans clanging, and all the voices of the ladies in the kitchen as we spoke. Now, I stood precisely in the same spot he did for all of those conversations.

Mike and David stayed in the front room talking to some of the boys in their broken, limited Spanish, and Clarita met some girls there who taught English or something. I stood by the kitchen with Julian, so overwhelmed, trying to take it all in. Words can't describe it.

I turned to Julian and hugged his neck. "I can't believe we're really here."

We hadn't even been in Colombia for twenty-four hours yet. When we finally left Juan David's house, David expressed feeling as overwhelmed as I did. We all felt the same. We walked across the busy street to catch a bus to take back to the apartment together. As we stepped away from the orphanage, our time as a family of four began.

Julian seemed incredibly nervous, but as we talked during the bus ride, he relaxed. He'd just left the orphanage to spend time with a family for the first time ever, never having experienced anything like this even once in his life before. He'd lived in this orphanage since the age of ten. His turn finally came to join a family, now as a young adult.

That night we planned to head to the Christian school's graduation like we arranged four months previously, the only event set on our calendar besides our upcoming meeting at the orphanage. We felt a bit awkward going to a graduation where we didn't know a soul, but we went with hopes of meeting several of the teachers and staff. So, after we left the orphanage, we went back to the apartment to let Julian drop off his stuff and accommodate himself.

Our little apartment offered a single bedroom and an office, a tiny kitchen, a living/dining area with a table, couch, futon, and two small bathrooms. David slept on the couch, so we gave Julian the option of sleeping on the futon across from him or taking the mattress off to sleep on the floor in the office. He chose the office.

We enjoyed our first meal with Julian at an Italian restaurant in the mall across the street from the apartment. He seemed more comfortable now that we stole a chance to sit and talk. I already felt like I had known him for a long time. Clarita asked many questions of us all, so the conversation never found a dry point while we all ate together.

Since Clarita worked at the Christian school when she first came to Colombia, she decided to go to the graduation with us in hopes of seeing some old friends (scratch out another fear of traveling somewhere we'd never gone without a guide). We enjoyed the ceremony, but Julian pointed out all the ways it differed from his own recent graduation from a public school.

Afterwards, Clarita introduced us to the director of the school and to many of the other teachers. We found it almost ironic when we realized Julian stood in the minority rather than us. Almost everyone from the school spoke English, many coming from America! At least Mike and David felt at ease for the evening. A few teachers invited us out for pizza later that evening, but we declined so we could head back to the apartment. This would be our first night with Julian, and quite frankly, we didn't know what to expect.

Back at the apartment, David and I dug out the games to break the ice. We brought several with us to teach Julian because we love to play games as a family. We picked out the ones that didn't require a lot of talking since a huge language barrier existed between David, Mike, and Julian.

We played Connect Four first, and it ended up being our favorite game. We played it like crazy. With no TV, Internet, or phone in the apartment, all the games came in handy. They forced us to communicate and spend a lot of quality time as a family.

After a few games of Connect Four that first night, Julian expressed his exhaustion and desire to turn in for the night. I wonder if he even slept the night before. I gave him a hug and told him I loved him before saying goodnight. Then he gave Mike a hug and said, "Goodnight, Dad." What a priceless moment.

David snuggled up beside me on his couch, and I read to him until he fell asleep. Then Mike and I went to bed, too. I would cherish this day in my heart for the rest of my life. We really did spend a day in Colombia, and God covered every last detail over our first thirty-six hours. Each moment seemed miraculous to me.

Later the next morning, Julian asked me what book I read to David the night before. I showed him a specific series of books and told him the basic theme of the books. Over the last year, I bid goodnight early to Julian via the computer so I could read to David before he fell asleep. Now he witnessed our story time with his own eyes.

Monday morning we met our second point of contact, our friend Rachel who we met online through the mission organization that sent us the "divine" brochure. She offered to accompany us to our meeting at the orphanage with the psychologist and social worker the following day to help with translation for Mike and David, but we still anticipated meeting her in person.

We all got up early to eat breakfast at the mall, and she met us there mid-morning. She told us all about herself and her ministry for street kids that she'd worked with in Colombia for the last seventeen years. What an amazing lady with a huge heart. I felt honored to meet her. She also met Julian, and our love and commitment to him touched her. She asked him a lot of questions about his story and his life, and she offered to connect him with her church and ministry after we left.

We decided to visit her ministry the next day and have lunch there with her before she headed to the orphanage with us later in the afternoon. She even drew us a little map with instructions to help us get there safely. Before leaving the mall that morning, she suggested several nice places to visit during our time in Colombia.

That same afternoon, we took her suggestion and spontaneously ventured out on our first tourist adventure with Julian. We headed to a famous place called Monserrate. Once we got there and purchased tickets, we squeezed into a little cable car that lifted us up to the top of a mountain where you could take pictures of the entire city from an aerial view. With our camera fully charged, we snapped picture after picture all the way up. What an inspiring view met us as we stepped out of the car at the top.

We glanced over the edge of the mountain to see all of Bogotá, a city of seven million people, spread out below us. On the other side, you could look down to see a beautiful landscape of mountains and valleys, an absolutely breathtaking view!

There we stood, now with Julian by our side, at the top of the mountain. It hit me. We'd made it. We survived the valley and made it back to the top of the mountain.

Julian may have seen his city spread out on one side and a beautiful landscape on the other. I saw so much more. As I looked out over the city, I saw a mission field filled with millions of lost souls needing a Savior. As I looked out over the valleys, I saw the valley we ourselves walked through. It no longer resembled the ugliness I saw when I walked through it, the distorted picture I grew accustomed to looking at.

The view of the valley took my breath away. I could finally see how intricately God worked together every tiny detail. The pieces of our puzzle all fit together without a single piece missing. I saw his fingerprints all over every hardship, wiping every tear away. I saw his footprints in every place he carried us. I saw his hands, guiding our every step. I saw his heart in the intimate love written all over an orphan's face. I saw his grace in Julian's beautiful smile.

We witnessed miracle after miracle before our eyes over the following thirteen days of our trip. Like watching a movie, we saw God plan out our every moment. Our meeting at the orphanage with the social worker and psychologist amazed us. They couldn't thank us enough for what we did for Julian.

"This whole experience is like a dream come true for Julian, a dream he never believed could actually come true this late in his life. He always wanted his siblings to find a family, but he thought it was already too late for him. Your relationship with him motivates him to keep trying to succeed in all he does." His psychologist explained how we became his driving force, taking on the inspiring role of parents.

Because Julian demonstrated such a gift in the arts and already accomplished so much academically for his age, they allowed him to stay longer so they could enroll him into college. In that meeting, we witnessed how hard his social worker pursued the best opportunities available for each individual child in her care.

Both the psychologist and social worker suddenly talked freely about the impact we also made on Juan David and Viviana. We did indeed matter. Although we no longer maintained contact with them, no one could erase the impact of the memories we built. That relationship mattered, and it had purpose.

I walked away so impressed by the support these three siblings received while in this orphanage. The very title that scared me the most, the psychologist, actually made us feel the most welcomed and appreciated with her warm, tender heart. In fact, she invited us to spend an entire day sight-seeing with her and her son as our guides, and later we enjoyed an authentic Colombian meal together at a famous restaurant near her hometown. No longer the feared psychologist, she quickly assumed the role of a dear friend. I will always remember her with very fond memories.

We arrived in Colombia still feeling like someone slapped us in the face for even thinking we could parent an adoptive child. Now we could leave Colombia feeling embraced and appreciated for changing an orphan's life and making his dreams come true. We also knew he changed our lives as much as we changed his, if not more.

During our two weeks in Colombia, we experienced one adventure after another. We visited Rachel's ministry, took lots of pictures, and we thanked God for the opportunity to expose Julian to this beautiful ministry in his own hometown. We visited the Christian school and met personally with the director to discuss future possibilities for our family to get involved in the ministry by using our own God-given gifts and talents. Julian never even heard of a missionary before, and now he had the opportunity to meet many of them.

We finally got in touch with the man who used to pastor the Spanish service at our church back home. As we spent a beautiful evening with him and his family, Julian witnessed what the family of Christ looks and acts like. Our friends even offered to take us to the airport for our flight home, also promising to get Julian back home safely after our departure. We knew basically no one before arriving in Colombia, but because we made so many contacts with fellow Christians on our journey, we gained many new friends, and they treated us like family.

We filled our days with adventure and ate out more than we should have. We got quite familiar with the mall, met a lot of people, and spent nearly every evening with Clarita and her roommate. But, more than anything, we spent time as a family, giving Julian the experience he missed over the last eight years. We made popcorn, curled up together on the futon, and watched movies on the laptop. We played games and held Connect Four tournaments. David and Julian, determined to play together, always found ways to communicate with their very limited Spanish and English.

Julian was eighteen years old, nine years older than David, yet he still resembled a child at heart. We learned in our pre-adoption training that an adopted child often needs to revert back to the age they lost their parent, making them need the affection a child of that age needs. Interestingly, that took Julian back to David's current age. No wonder they both got along and connected so well. No wonder he took so quickly to the affection we naturally showed him.

Julian warmed up quickly. After the first two nights, he stopped sleeping alone in the office. Instead, he stayed up late listening to me read to David, though not understanding a word, before he fell asleep on the futon right across from David. When he didn't listen to me read, he read a little New Testament in Spanish he found in the office, the only reading material he could find in Spanish.

We shared many long talks, usually in the mornings while Mike and David slept in. I found out he met Christ at the age of nine. He could explain the gospel clearly and understood it well. Now, he read scripture every night and then explained what he read, showing me how well he understood it. God so evidently worked in his life all these years. He just needed someone to guide him in his spiritual growth.

We prayed together at all of our meals, so much that Julian would remind us if we forgot to say the prayer. We cooked and cleaned together every day and gave hugs and kisses every night. I can't even begin to count the times he stopped, looked at me with a huge smile, and told me how much he loved being with us. We had become a family, his family. He finally found where he belonged.

Sadly, our fourteen days together came to an end, and we had to say good-bye. Our mountaintop experience finished, and our life with Julian, now as a family of four, began. We left with the promise to help him financially whenever he had to leave the orphanage, or to pay for all of his expenses if he's ever able to get a visa to study in the States. His legal support team said they would help him with the process to pursue that opportunity. They reminded us that the material help didn't compare to the affective bond we established with him.

His social worker said she'd stay in contact with us to keep us involved in any decisions made for his future. He finally got accepted into an art college and started a few weeks later, while we returned to our own home and places of work.

We continue to call and write Julian each week, as well as find an occasional time to communicate via a Skype call on the computer. We helped him out with his bus fare to go to school and with all of the art supplies he needed for his classes. He sends us pictures of his completed projects in return. We're still praying diligently, asking God if, when, or for how long he wants us to return to Colombia. For now, we plan to go back in the summer to spend time with Julian again, and to actually work at the Christian school doing short-term missions.

So, we'll see how God leads from here.

(I remember saying that exact thing when Julian suddenly appeared in our lives . . . you never know what God has up his sleeve.)

I jumped into teaching yet another ladies' Bible study at church for the summer, literally two days after coming home from Colombia. I led a new group of ladies through a Women of Faith workbook study called *Hope—The Anchor for Your Soul*.[9] Pretty fitting, I thought. For the first time, I found myself on the other side of hope, having watched my hope become a reality.

I started my next study in the fall, Beth Moore's DVD study called "The Inheritance."[10] We learned together how God entrusts every experience to us as a part of our inheritance. Sometimes he just tells us to grab hold of his hand and hold on as tightly as we can because he will see us through it, through every unexpected tear along the way.

That describes our story in a nutshell.

Each study I teach brings new women into my life I might never have known. In fact, God brought a certain lady to my study that first night in the fall who just happened to have grown up as a missionary child in—Bogotá, Colombia!

This story keeps getting better!

God did indeed give me the desires of my heart, the ones I wrote in my letter to him at the beginning of the spring Bible study, even down to the printing of this book. Little did I know while I wrote of my desire to write a book, I actually lived out the details of the story he wanted me to write.

My last request in that letter asked God to turn our story around to give us a story only he could author. As to whether or not he did that, I'll let you, the reader, be the judge.

Epilogue
HOW WOULD I KNOW?

This story documents our journey to Julian, someone we will always love as our son even if we can never officially adopt him. He calls us Mom and Dad, and he refers to our biological son as his brother—interestingly, a brother the same age as the little sister he lost and with the same interests and passions as his younger brother who will soon be adopted away from him.

This story also demonstrates God's love for the orphan. Julian embraced the opportunity to start college for at least a semester, and he definitely became quite the artist. Juan David plays on a soccer team, and Viviana now has a teacher for a mom. God did not abandon any of them, but he instead placed them each with a family who could meet their individual needs. (In addition to his provision for these three siblings, God also led the couple we sat with at the Adoption Conference to domestically adopt their daughter, while my new friend from the El Salvador online group eventually adopted four siblings from South America.)

However, this book also reveals my own journey of faith, intimately describing how God broke me, molded me, taught me, and guided me along the way through our entire "adoption" experience. Our story travels through grief and loss, hope and healing, obedience and trust, and God's ever sufficient grace. It follows a family trudging through an adoption process and then trying to survive the valley when that adoption never came to fruition.

I learned more about Christ and grew closer to him throughout this particular journey than any other time in my life. I cried so many unexpected tears. Tears of waiting. Tears of grief. Tears of joy. Yet if he never led me through the valley, there is so much about him I would never know. When I finally reached the top of the mountain and looked back over the valley, I could almost hear God gently whisper in my ear.

"See, my child? Didn't I tell you it would be worth it? Didn't I tell you the view would take your breath away?"

If I had never been there, I could not know what I do now. Experiencing Colombia itself didn't take our breath away, but the spiritual journey getting there did. As I look back down over the valley we traveled, and recall God's obvious footprints beside each of my own, I realize I found the greatest beauty of all.

Scripture tells us he is our great reward. I may not have gotten the two children I set out to adopt, but I got so much more.

I got him.

Nothing else, in all of life, can compare.

How Would I know?

How would I know of your provision
if I never found myself in desperate need?

How would I know of your healing
if I didn't see you heal my bitter heart?

How would I know of your restoration
if my life never crumbled before my eyes?

How would I know you are my refuge
if I never wanted to run away and hide?

How would I know of your constancy
if I never watched my dreams slip away?

How would I know of Divine Guidance
if I never found myself utterly lost?

How would I know of your hope

if I never felt all hope was gone?
How would I know of your comfort
if I never felt such crushing pain?

How would I see your light
if I never had to walk in the dark?

How would I know you hold me together
if I never lost every ounce of strength I had?

How would I know of your redemption
if I never lost something so close to my heart?

How would I know of your power
if I never needed nothing short of a miracle?

How would I know you alone can satisfy
if I never felt such an incredible void?

How would I know you are the answer
if I never had to search so frantically for one?

How would I know you are always with me
if I never felt completely alone?

How would I know I could trust you
if I never had to take a leap of faith?

How would I know I could confide in you
if you never had to wipe away my tears?

How would I know how much I need you
if I never felt I couldn't take another step?

How would I know you like I know you now

if you never allowed me to go through these trials?
How would I understand inexplicable JOY
if I never felt it amidst the deepest heartache?

How would I know how to carry others' burdens
if no one ever had to carry mine?

How would I know the testimony you gave me
if you never put me through a test?

How would I know I could love you
if you never passionately pursued my heart?

How would I know you could sustain me
if I never found myself too weak to survive?

How would I know how much you love me
if you never gave your life for me?

How would I know who you are
if I never had to find out?

How would I know of your constant grace
if I never shed so many unexpected tears?

How could I see the beauty of the valley
if I'd never been to the mountain and back with you?

"Look! I see another mountaintop from here! It's even more beautiful than this one!" The possibility tempted me, but I couldn't deny the huge valley separating us from the beauty.
    Did we dare?

Appendix
A LIFE WITH PURPOSE

As you read about my family's journey through a painful adoption experience, I hope you gleaned an even deeper message written between the lines of our story. *Nothing matters more than a personal relationship with Jesus Christ.*

Living through a "failed" adoption happened to be the circumstance God used in our lives to show us that he never leaves us, whether we find ourselves on the mountaintop or in the valley. He fills our lives with meaning and purpose. He satisfies our hearts when we stop looking everywhere else for fulfillment.

If you read through my story and felt drawn to begin your own relationship with Christ, please know you can do so at this very moment. *Call out to him. Admit your need for him. Surrender your life to him.* We all fall short of his glory, but Jesus Christ (God's son) already paid the price for the sins that separated us from him. His salvation is a gift, one we can never earn, no matter how hard we try. We can't fix ourselves on our own, but if we give our life to him, he does the fixing, drawing us closer and closer to himself to make us more like him.

By confessing our sin, admitting we need a Savior, and giving our life to Jesus, we can enter into a relationship with the God who created us. We can find assurance that he will prepare a place for us in Heaven for eternity, but we can also find an abundant and meaningful life here and now. A life with purpose.

Imagine a life with such an awesome relationship. I can't even begin to imagine a life without it. Without him.

How can I begin a relationship with God?

Believe the following:
- Christ makes us a new creation. "Therefore, if anyone is in

Christ, he is a new creation. The old has passed away; behold, the new has come" (2 Cor. 5:17, ESV). Tell God you want him to change you into a new creation to bring honor to him.

- God forgives our sins and allows us a new start. "Blessed are those whose lawless deeds are forgiven, and whose sins are covered" (Rom. 4:7, ESV). Let God know you know you are a sinner and want his forgiveness.
- He grants us eternal life. "For God so loved the world, that he gave his only Son, that whoever believes in him should not perish but have eternal life" (John 3:16, ESV). Ask God to give you eternal life by allowing you into his family.
- God gives us indescribable joy. "Though you have not seen him, you love him. Though you do not now see him, you believe in him and rejoice with joy that is inexpressible and filled with glory, obtaining the outcome of your faith, the salvation of your souls" (1 Pet. 1:8–9). This doesn't promise happiness, but joy in knowing Christ as your personal savior, and hope that he manages the details of our lives for his glory.
- We can begin talking to God about all aspects of our life. We can ask him to show us which paths to take or what decisions to make, and start communicating even the tiny details of our lives with him. But let's not forget to listen. God wants to speak back.
- God talks to us through the Bible, so start reading his message to you. Websites such as BibleGateway.com or YouVersion.com offer a variety of translations free of charge. I recommend beginning with the Gospel of John or one of the other Gospels to learn what Jesus taught during his time on earth.
- Authenticity Book House would love to hear about your decision to follow Christ.
- E-mail us at info@abhbooks.com. We would love to pray for you and celebrate with you the new life you have in Christ.

MORE IN THE SURVIVING THE VALLEY SERIES

Just a few months after Rachelle D. Alspaugh finished writing *Unexpected Tears*, it became apparent that her story wasn't over. Follow Rachelle as God takes her on yet another trek of faith through the valley on her journey toward international adoption. *Painful Waiting* picks up where *Unexpected Tears* leaves off. Will the path lead her family back to Colombia? What beauty might await them at the top of the next mountain?

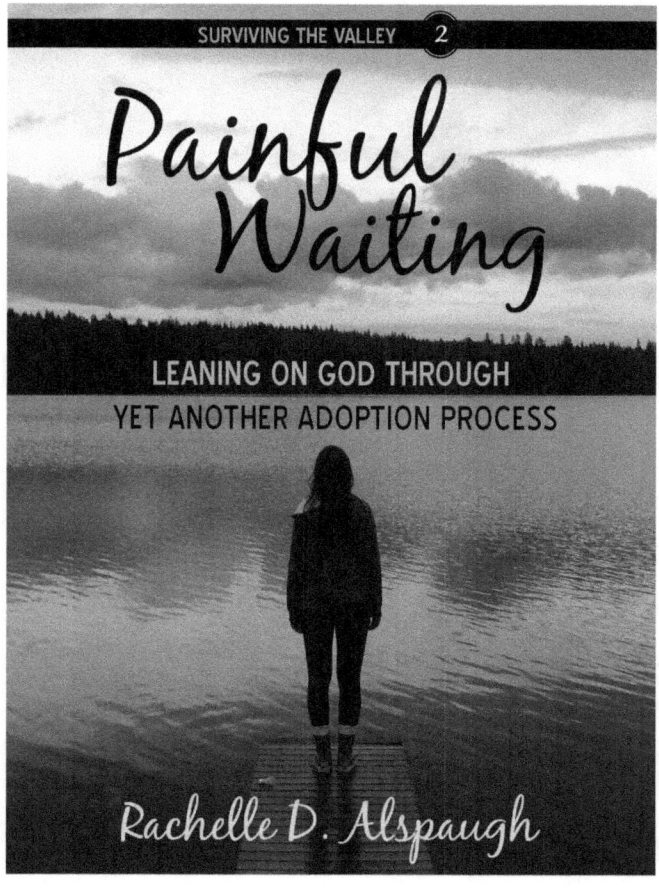

Endnotes

1. "Resurrection," Nicol Sponberg, 2007, Curb Records.
2. *The Power of a Praying Wife*, Stormie Omartian, 1997, Harvest House Publishers.
3. *Extraordinary Faith*, Sheila Walsh, 2005, Thomas Nelson.
4. *The Grace of Catastrophe—When What You Know About God is All You Have*, Jan Winebrenner, 2005, Moody Publishers.
5. *Dream Giver*, Bruce Wilkinson, 2003, Multnomah Books.
6. *Wild Goose Chase—Reclaim the Adventure of Pursuing God*, Mark Batterson, 2008, Multnomah Books.
7. *Walking by Faith—Lessons I Learned in the Dark*, Jennifer Rothschild, 2003, Life Way Press.
8. *Beloved Disciple*, Beth Moore, 2002, Life Way Press.
9. *Hope—The Anchor* for Your Soul, Women of Faith, 2004, Thomas Nelson.
10. *The Inheritance*, DVD Bible Study Series, Beth Moore, 2010, Living Proof Ministries.

About the Author

Rachelle D. Alspaugh seldom finds herself at a loss for words when she writes. She tells stories about faith, and her poetry often springs from real events in her life.

Rachelle yearns to help orphans. She enjoys traveling, especially when her travels intersect with her passion for missions. In college, she went to Buenos Aires for a semester as an exchange student. She also spent two months in Mexico as a summer missionary, and has taken several mission trips to Mexico since.

Rachelle teaches Bilingual Education in a public school system just outside of Dallas, Texas, where she lives with her husband and two sons, along with their two dogs and two cats. She also enjoys teaching women's Bible studies at her church.

www.ingramcontent.com/pod-product-compliance
Lightning Source LLC
LaVergne TN
LVHW051052080426
835508LV00019B/1827